This Way Up

This Way Up

A Faith-Based Introduction to Jordan Peterson's 'Maps of Meaning'

Annette Poizner

LOBSTER UNIVERSITY PRESS
TORONTO, CANADA

Contents

Introduction

"It was the best of times, it was the worst of times, it was the age of wisdom, it was the age of foolishness, it was the path of belief, it was the path of incredulity, it was the season of Light, it was the season of Darkness, it was the spring of hope, it was the winter of despair"

Charles Dickens

Charles Dickens words resonate with me these days, especially with the terrible strife facing the world, the eruption of the Corona virus and the havoc it is playing in our lives. But I have to hang on to the positive, too: an awakening at play. My Facebook feed, serving up posts from the Jordan Peterson groups that convene, has been showing me tendrils of growth for some time now, from a younger generation whose secularism was formerly indisputable.

I have been listening in on people coming of age. LR wondered if anybody would like to go to church with him. He wrote, "I was raised Catholic and rejected it at an early age. Over the past 10 years and especially through the work of Peterson, I'm finally starting to be able to separate the wheat from the chaff." AC shared a predicament: "I have been a staunch, Richard Dawkins-esque atheist since I was about 15 and learned what the word meant (I'm 25 now). After listening to and absorbing JP's teachings, as well as other people of history, I realize I'm a strong believer in Christianity whether or not I take the Bible literally." She has been struggling. "What is there for me, a nonbeliever believer?" She would love to join a church and befriend other Christians but doesn't know how to find her place in the world of organized religion when biblical literalism doesn't speak to her. Someone else asked "is there a reliable way of finding a local church that is friendly to JBP's ideas?" Another post was earnest in its simplicity: "How can I know G-d?"

My sense is that this awakening is not limited to any one religion. Twenty years ago a 16-year-old local, the kid down the street, wore his hair gelled into very long protruding cones. I paid him to mow my lawn. He was far from non-descript as he did so. He found his place in the downtown artistic community and became active in the social justice movement. His bed-fellows were left-wing. Fast forward: His kitchen is kosher, he is active in the Jewish community. Now he aspires to marry and build a Jewish family. He tells me the ideas of Jordan Peterson prompted an awakening, a shift.

And then there are some who, independent of religious sentiments, are documenting massive life changes. WA has been making progress reports every few months. He's lost 32 pounds, working out regularly, noticing fitness improvements and psychological benefits. He feels stronger and more assertive. Despite a history of trauma his anxiety symptoms have improved. His wife is now undertaking her health journey. He posts his 'before' and 'after' pictures and then asks, "have you found JP to be helpful in your life in a similar way? What have you been able to do with what you've learned?" There are 152 comments. The community celebrates his success and shares stories.

Change is afoot. What's great about the Jordan Peterson phenomenon is that there is a whole generation who are rethinking their premises and engaging with classical ideas that have shaped societies over thousands of years. Peterson has revivified the relevance of those ideas. But don't take it from me. Visit YouTube and check out the bible lectures that he gave back in 2017. More specifically, check out the comments:

"About a year ago, I clicked this video. This series changed my life. Thank you, Mr. Peterson. And best of luck to anyone starting their journey."

"Clean house by day, JP podcast by night."

"Thanks for your uploads Jordan. I'm a 46-year-old shipwreck that is slowly but surely repairing itself thanks to you."

And, in response to the endless stream of comments that pay homage to Peterson and his work, another: "Can I be friends with you people? Where are you?? Why can I not find people who adore these videos in my physical proximity?"

There are thousands of such comments. The last comment mentioned, though, is exactly to the point. Young people need to find community, need a venue for discussing what they have learned from Peterson and an address where they can learn more. Now, facing new stresses prompted by dramatic world changes, they need an anchor in faith and spirituality, now more than ever. Can Peterson's ideas help people in these times, characterized by terrible turbulence and uncertainty?

Building a Bridge

On one hand, I'm writing this book to directly address those for whom secularism has been their only path, those who sense they may need a deeper anchor to withstand the turbulence that clearly awaits us. Additionally, I'm writing this book to help the faith communities understand what Peterson has been teaching so they will better understand the young people who will be walking through their doors for the first time. Understanding these modern-day seekers is the first step to programing for them or conversing with them.

Additionally, I've prepared this book because I suspect that those with a faith-orientation will appreciate an orientation to Peterson's work that has been prepared from a faith perspective. Peterson's ideas can be useful to those of all faiths, but some may need to understand some of his core ideas viewed through the lens of faith, for starters, so they can then decide whether to delve further into his work.

I'm writing this book, then, to summarize some of Peterson's important concepts, his worldview, his ideas about the structure of the mind, the psychological necessity of the G-d ideal, the nature of Reality and its constituent aspects of chaos and order. I'm summarizing his insights about the map of meaning that each person must create, a map which can and should be informed by maps that have proven their viability over the centuries, maps put forward by monotheistic religions; maps which remain available today to seekers who are looking for answers.

My Story

And now a little about me. I have been a Jordan Peterson enthusiast for some time now, introduced to his work by a young male psychotherapy client who took inspiration and direction from his lectures. I was curious. I listened, read and found wisdom in many of Peterson's ideas. I occasionally recommended these lectures to my clients. I harboured a thought: somebody really should write a summary of Peterson's *Maps of Meaning: The Architecture of Belief.*

One day – naively – I sent out a glowing email about Peterson and his journaling program to a group of local social workers who chat about professional issues. The response I received was dramatic. Peterson, they agreed – in unison – was a modern day Jim Jones, spreader of hate, etc, etc. I decided not to post any further about Peterson's work on that chat group. If this feedback was any indicator, clients motivated by Peterson might be hard-pressed to find a therapist who admired his work. I was angry about that. But I put the issue aside. Until March, 2019.

On February 22, a really snowy, icy Toronto day, I donned my snow gear to meet psychotherapy clients in my downtown office. I parked at the subway, then trudging to the station, had a fleeting thought: "in my late 50's, I still have fight left in me, bearing the elements like this!" Within seconds of registering that idea, I wiped out on ice, broke two bones in my ankle, dislocated my foot and reconfigured my agenda. Surgery and couch living was going to be life for the next while. The next long while.

Now I needed a project. I remembered the social workers scathing comments about Peterson. Many in those ranks are 'social justice warriors'. I remembered my thoughts about Peterson's scholarly tome. So why don't I try to put together a practical summary of his book? *A Practical Summary & Workbook for Using Jordan Peterson's Insights to Sort Yourself Out* was born, published by my imprint, Lobster University Press. My task was to omit mythology, ditch the brain science and stick to the meat of the issue (no pun intended given Peterson's diet), as I, a long time psychotherapist, perceived it: articulate the most important ideas here that can help people understand reality and themselves; the ideas that can help people make important changes.

As I was writing the book, I had to catch myself. My own perspective is informed by my faith. I constantly reminded myself to stay true to Peterson's text. A practical summary would make Peterson's work more accessible to many and it was not my task to insert references to faith, so I didn't.

In the course of sharing the work with other Peterson fans, though, I came to see that there is a bona fide need to put out a different book: one that specifically speaks to the interests and orientation of those who harbour an awareness of G-d, those who navigate a relationship with Him within one of the world's religions. Why? Because Peterson argues the case for faith, he shows the troubles that accrue those devoid of the G-d ideal but he otherwise leaves followers to find their own path to transcendence. Rightly so. It is not for him to proselytize or advance any given religion. Each must go their own way.

It's the job of clergy and religious educators to pick up where Peterson leaves off. Or it's the job of seekers, themselves. I hope that readers will find in this document a starter kit to Peterson and his material. I look forward to input from readers that will allow me to improve this document. When it comes to summarizing Peterson, I have to admit the task is beyond me! The benefit of this mode of publishing is that the medium is forgiving. I continue to tweak my work with the sage input of many wonderful readers.

My Format

I have chosen a specific format for sharing this material. I decided to reprint several chapters from my original volume, those sections highlighting what I understand to be Peterson's core premises, and intersperse these with italicized comments that provide context, background or ideas of interest to those in the faith communities. This format allows me to make distinctions between the ideas that are more authentically Peterson's and those which I cull from other sources and use to illuminate issues relating to faith. In the first chapter I am summarizing what I understand to be Peterson's worldview.

The second chapter[1] provides a detailed summary of Peterson's thoughts about the psychological significance of the G-d ideal. You won't find too many italicized sections here.

The third chapter details the phenomenon of the Map of Meaning, providing Peterson's insights but also those of other theorists – like Alfred Adler – who had much to say on the map and how it is shaped. The fourth chapter presents what I call Peterson's Map of Meaning. We look at many of his 'rules' and concepts, revisiting some ideas from the first chapter but positioning them so we look at the reality landscape as a whole in tandem with his best advice for living within it. I present some of Peterson's ideas juxtaposed to insights that emerge when we study the Creation narrative in the Hebrew Bible. Doing so helps up appreciate the comprehensive nature of his work and advice.

My task was to produce a resource that would facilitate readers' comprehension of Peterson's text. I have outlined important ideas found in the first two chapters of that book. The feedback I've received so far is that this material helps readers better understand Peterson's framework of ideas. You can let me know if you agree or whether you have ideas for improvement.

I will explain that my own path is Orthodox Judaism. My aim here is to discuss Divinity in general terms to, I hope, speak to those of diverse backgrounds and denominations. In keeping with the Jewish tradition, I will be avoiding fully spelling the English term for Divinity. The Jewish faith prohibits the full spelling of any Divine name lest that document be scrapped, an affront to the holiness encoded in any name that denotes the sacred. But, aside from this stricture, I feel that there is something apropos in forgoing the full spelling. Each reader must find their their own spelling, their own unique relationship with the ineffable Divinity at the root of creation, a discovery that may correspond to their heritage or, otherwise, their destiny.

"It Was the Best of Times, It Was the Worst of Times"

Dennis Prager has offered an interesting reflection. American records of mass shootings over the decades show a very specific trend. There were no such shootings in the 1950's, but the number of shootings in each decade thereafter rose, gradually and steadily, becoming more frequent with each passing decade. In earlier years, Prager asserts, protocols to access guns were similar to those of today. Prager speculates that the rising number of shootings relates, then, not to easier access to guns but to a decline in religiosity. When religiosity diminishes, so do inhibitions; Prager hypothesizes that men in particular need the archetype of G-d. That archetype encourages healthy ways of channeling testosterone, the male hormone that gets men into trouble as per the research cited by Peterson. Toss the ideal and civility goes with it.

Peterson is fueling a resurgence of interest in the G-d ideal. There is a cadre of young people who are contemplating a return, revisiting the religious ways of their ancestors. If this trend continues, perhaps society will reinstate the centrality and importance of that ideal. If this consciousness continues to waft over us, perhaps, gradually, healthy inhibitions will again take root across the board. Could new norms emerge? Less acceptance of crude language as normative? More religiousity among the mainstream? More interest in religious ritual and attendance at places of worship? Less sexualization of absolutely everything? How about a decade where the number of public shootings actually dips? Can we reinstate some of the innocence and piety associated with days gone by?

It's a vision of progress that is idealized in prayers around the world. I'll end with one that I know:

And on that day He will be proclaimed King of all the land

And on that day there will be one G-d

And His name will be One

Notes

1. The second chapter is adapted from another book that I recently published called *An Illustrated Guide for Using Jordan Peterson's Insights Regarding Divinity & the Map of Meaning to Sort Yourself Out.*

1.

An Introduction to Jordan Peterson's Worldview

In the first chapter, our task is to work sequentially through Jordan Peterson's worldview as he states it in the first two chapters of the "Maps of Meaning" text and related lectures. The chapter consists of sections in regular font and those in italics. In the regular font, you will read synopses of Peterson's premises and the arguments he makes to defend them. In the italics, you will read commentary offered from a faith-based perspective. The idea is to bridge his strictly psychological perspective with a sensibility that registers the sacred which, I suggest, will be a starting point for better understanding Peterson fans who are exploring matters of faith.

What is reality?

What is reality? Peterson suggests that your basic premises about reality, likely influenced by the way that science has advanced our lives, may be wrong.

Based on what you see, you might conclude that ours is a world of things. Objects are comprised of atoms or molecules. Cells are the constituent part of people and animals. Sound breaks down into sound waves and so on. So we think, as per the discoveries of science, that our world is, first and foremost, physical. In fact, our worldview is so influenced by science that the idea is pervasive: things are the stuff of life. Ours is a world of things.

Not so fast. Peterson points out that, despite our first impressions, we live in a world of value. Whenever we see some facet of the physical world, what 'is' exists alongside 'what could be'.

If you're an interior designer, you walk into a room and note the decoration but in your mind's eye you quickly come up with your vision of a better layout, furniture that would be better in this space. The judge who watches the Olympic athlete sees the athletic performance and compares it in the minds' eye to what the most ideal performance would look like. That internally generated standard will determine whether the athlete gets a medal and, if so, which medal. A seasoned cook tastes the food and, comparing the taste to the standard that exists in the 'inner palette', knows which spices to add.

Duality of the World

Peterson's starting point is this interesting duality that sits at the core of our experience of the world. That duality is addressed by mystics in various traditions. Here I will summarize some premises of Jewish mysticism.

According to Kabbalah, the world is wholly comprised of Divinity. To facilitate creation, G-d made a vacuum or 'cavity' within Himself to accommodate creation much like a womb accommodates a fetus. G-d then formed the various facets of creation out of his own essence, a process partly described in Genesis.[1] *Certain creations, such as the angels, all formed from lofty emanations, would, by necessity, be strongly conscious of Divinity. Flooded with awareness of the G-dly reality, accessing the meaning that underpins creation, such a being single-mindedly intones hymns, paying endless homage to the Divinity that sits at the core of reality.*

G-d's master purpose in creating the world, though, was to produce a being with a capacity for near perfection which the being, itself, could choose to either bring to fruition or degrade. To achieve an environment which allowed either of these outcomes, G-d would have to hide Himself within creation. Only by masking the Divine root of the world and its premise of justice and goodness would humans be truly free to choose either path. Why? In the face of obvious Divinity, a being could do none other than choose the path of goodness (Tatz, 1995). So G-d created a physical reality which appears to have its own independent existence. Now the world has a certain look to it. It looks like a world of things that have an independent existence of their own. These things seem set. They seem to constitute reality.

Of course, creating what appears to be a void of Divinity and so reconfiguring or partly filtering out the Divinity which otherwise would perfume the world with obvious goodness, creates the possibility for evil. Peterson will talk at length about this evil, evil which people can rightly find in themselves, locating and recognizing it, monitoring and controlling it. This sensibility – that evil exists and we necessarily find it within ourselves – is foreign to secular psychology but a premise of the religious worldview. Peterson's contribution of this idea, alone, does a lot of good. People don't have to explain away negative aspects of their personalities as a function of old wounds or the necessary fault of others, poor upbringing, etc. We get to assume responsibility for modulating the negativity we rightly and appropriately find within. In fact, we get to rise to the challenge of locating our evil, modulating it and even alchemically morphing it into something more useful. The result of that project: a life of meaning. As Peterson says:

> *Being is suffering tainted by malevolence and, so, what's the meaning? There's pain to alleviate. There's chaos to confront. And there's order to establish and revivify and there's evil to constrain, not least in our own hearts and that's meaning enough for everyone.*

Another important point: Divinity hides giving the superficial impression of being absent but, G-d, de facto, leaves clues indicating His actual Presence. He remains deep and fundamentally engaged with creation, fundamentally embedded within it. That fact was noticed by Moses when he beheld the burning bush, or by Abram when he initially surmised the existence of G-d (as recounted in Midrash) and destroyed his father's idols. In other words, the Creator can be found within his creation by those with searching eyes. G-d hides in nature, hoping to be found.

If humans were created with the same Divine infrastructure of angels, they would see Divinity clearly, which would prove a barrier to free will. Therefore, humans would be created with deficiencies which each could struggle to reverse, or appease and so worsen. In other words, each person could quest to resolve deficiencies, aiming at the elusive goal of restoring the Divinity within and, with gradual progress would earn an ever-improving connection with/awareness of Divinity. Devoting life to the task of repairing deficiencies would have a person properly bringing forward innate potential and promoting the better good, all around. Such a person, we might say, is sorting themselves out and continues to sort themselves out, as a lifestyle. They experience better health; the Divine spark descends and indwells in the body with less barrier. They radiate a certain brightness, a spirituality, too. The light of the Divine shines out in the eyes, teaches Chinese Medicine. This is a person, even an elderly person, who has a sparkle in the eyes. Not to say that a person ever achieves the state of perfection they may quest for. The project fills a lifetime and challenges or curve-balls make the process tricky. This, then, is the stuff of life.

> *The smallest good act today is the capture of a strategic point from which, a few months later, you may be able to go on to victories you never dreamed of.*
>
> *CS Lewis*

Now some people will avoid the heavy lifting involved in addressing deficiencies. They, instead, succumb to deficiencies.

tripping themselves into a vicious cycle of failure, falling, at each stage, to lower levels of depravity, resulting in distance from G-d. That outcome would be characterized by negativity, nihilism and hate. Resolving deficiencies, in contrast, would allow the human to access a supernal awareness of life's meaning as the G-dly perspective which man becomes privy to contains no less then the ultimate meaning that is encoded in creation. in some sense. Man would have the choice to choose progress or its opposite, in virtually every minute of existence, in every realm of life.

Given a soul rooted in Divinity, that soul would yearn for perfection, hungering for a return to the perfected state of unity with the Divine, the ultimate source of perfection. This yearning would fuel a drive to self-perfect, motoring a push for progress. When this motivation is expressed properly, unhindered by corrupting influences, it creates the impulse to act and improve self and world. Acting in the service of this impulse has the human mimicking his Creator. Such a person, fueled by ambition and determination, is rightly living not in a world defined by things, but in a world defined by action. Peterson spends time proving that the world of things perceived by our senses misleads us. That world is a mirage, designed to hide the Divinity that permeates creation. In reality, he asserts, the world is a world of action.

And action can be expressed in a range of directions. Actions can be purposeful and progressive. But any natural and healthy motivation can also be corrupted. When this occurs, the drive for progress regresses into a drive for self-gratification. Freud called that destructive impulse the death instinct. When the impulse to act is misdirected, action is deployed to indulge cravings; the world of action becomes mired in negativity, creating a scenario like that associated with the Flood. The commentaries assert that G-d flooded the world because action, at that time, was consistently malevolent. Even the animals and their mating behaviours had become pathological ("all flesh had corrupted its way," Genesis 6:12).

We see that the possibility of progress always hangs in the balance, very much contingent on the choices and decisions that each person makes on a moment by moment basis, determining how energies are channeled and towards what end, positive or negative. We will see in our lives that there can be a virtuous cycle, wherein one good action leads to another, or a vicious cycle, wherein one negative act leads to another, and so on and so forth.

Now we understand why it seems like we are in a world of things but why, Peterson stresses, we are more accurately living in a world of value and action.

A dichotomy, therefore, exists in how you experience your own life. In any moment, you have a current reality and you have goals. If you're in university, you are sitting in a classroom taking notes, but you are directed to your meta-outcome: graduating and getting a good job. You don't live in the present moment with the conception of yourself and your life as perfect as is. You have a number of goals you are working towards. Hopefully you retain those goals at the front of your mind at all times. So you live in the present and in the future, simultaneously.

In any moment, you perceive the physical reality, the mask of nature, but your Divinity is simultaneously expressed by the craving you have for progress (an urge to perfect). You want to achieve the next goal. Each accomplishment perfects you, allows you better expression of your innate Divinity. Over time and with effort, the choreography of your life is in synch with the Divinity at the root of creation. When you cooperate with the higher good, you feel better. Even if you are not conscious of a specific relationship with Divinity, you are buoyed by better access to your own Divine nature and are a beneficiary of improved Divine flow or blessing which plays out in the guise of synchronicities, a good mood or good outcomes that come of your efforts. You uncover the matrix of meaning that underpins creation as you participate with Divinity in the perfecting of that creation.

If the current state of anything is incomplete without a vision of what it could become, then the real nature of the world is action; a series of actions will be required to bring anyone/anything to an improved state. And science can't help us figure out the exact actions that will help any given person move forward, given his or her unique situation. Science helps us understand the objective world, but it deliberately removes the subjective element. Yet, it is the subjective element that we must mull over to come up with the unique life path for each of us.

Note the beginning of Genesis. Creation would seem to address a lack. There was nothing, and something needed to be created. We are comprised of Divinity. G-d is, therefore, our role model. The first report relates to his bold and decisive action. He creates the world! We emulate Divinity. We are here to act – purposefully – to step into the role of hero and bring good things into existence. The world is not a world of things. The world of things is the venue for the real purpose of life: action!

The Importance of the Map

According to Peterson, to the degree that individuals cobble together a useful map for themselves, aiming themselves towards appropriate outcomes and taking reasonable actions to move forward, is the degree to which they will experience meaning in life. To the degree that individuals' maps are poorly conceived and aim them badly, they flounder, feel depressed and are prone to negativity. After all, daily life is peppered with bad news, tragedy, illness. If there is no vision of productive action which could improve things, the present is unchanging; hopeless. At worse, people become nihilistic, negative about life itself.

Therefore, the various monotheistic religions are here to help, each providing a map of life. Spiritual traditions presume to offer a map that adherents can access and use to shape their own personal and unique map of meaning. Why? Because your car comes with operating instructions but your life does not. And therefore each person is forced to come up with some sort of map they will use to guide themselves forward. Growing up in a secular society means people are not exposed to a value-based, time-tested map. Peterson is helping create a consciousness amongst young people that this is something they have been missing: influence from sacred traditions which could help them flesh out their own personal map of meaning. When the personal map of meaning resonates with a sacred map, that which contains ideas that carry down from tried and true traditions, ideas that emphasize personal responsibility and the priority of goodness, this person is on the right track.

As Peterson says, "you need a path that justifies the tragedy of life." The right motivation allows you to strive, to force forward in a way that suits you, allowing you to undertake well chosen behaviors designed to improve things, regardless of challenges. A lot is going to ride on whether the map of life of any given individual serves the person or is somehow flawed and problematic. Clearly each person should take stock of his or her own map of life, even though it is implicit and not always easy to access. Peterson is introducing this priority to a generation of young people, and, in so doing, helping them change and upgrade outdated old maps that date back to childhood.

"We'll preserve for our children this, the last best hope of man on earth,
or we'll sentence them to take the last step into a thousand years of darkness."
Abraham Lincoln

If you have watched Peterson discussing Genesis, you may recall that he presented the story of Cain and Abel as the first narrative that relates to the normal human. Peterson reflects that Adam and Eve were not born in the usual manner so could not be called human in the usual sense. Peterson discusses the scenario that unfolds with Cain killing his brother. Cain will shape his future based on how he responds to his own sin. Will he dust off and try again, thereby committing to action and improvement? Or will he angrily fester?

In that passage, G-d warns Cain that a destructive response to sin will lead to his downfall. There's that teaching: that a person can choose a progressive or destructive frame in which to interpret and respond to events. With that message, G-d is trying to imprint Cain's map of meaning – and that of all of us. A person rises or falls contingent on how he or she deals with failure and the Bible will encourage us to shape our map with an awareness of this fact. We are to always choose an attitude that favours action versus collapsing into negativity and blame. Made with Divinity, we can choose the strategy put forward by Divinity, itself, to deal with tough moments.

So, to summarize, the elementary grammar of this world is the verb, not the noun. Ours is, first and foremost, a world of action which means that in any moment we need to figure out what to do to move life forward. We each, therefore, come up with a life map to guide the way and answer the myriad of questions that arise about how to move forward. What's the next step? How do I improve my life? Do I do what feels right or what sounds right? Right according to who? There are infinite visions, so many ways I can move. How do I figure out which way achieves the best outcome? My map will be a composite of all the answers that I generate in response to these, and other, questions.

The Known and the Unknown

Peterson adds another complexity that makes the task of living yet more confusing. There are two aspects to the world. There is the known world and the unknown world. Imagine a baby is born. Initially, the world itself, the crib, the nursery, the other children in the family and even the parents, exist as a mass of confusion for a baby that can't interpret the blur of sound, feeling and image. The baby is born into a world full of lights, sounds, stimuli – it's chaos!

That baby is ill-equipped to detect and interpret all the patterns embedded in this complex landscape.

As the brain and body of the baby is gradually able to read patterns and otherwise begin mapping out reality, mother's face becomes familiar. That face corresponds, say, to positive outcomes. Baby smiles when she sees that face. Gradually the map expands. Other facets of that murky, confusing world become intelligible. This is brother. This is sister. More associations. As a child learns to talk, to write, aspects of the unknown world become known. Those letters that used to look like unintelligible black shapes now are discerned as parts of words. Those markings make sense now. For the child, life has moved from an experience of chaos to one of order.

When years later she takes algebra, at the beginning of that course, she knows how to read, but all those letters and formulas look like a mash of nonsense. By the end of the course, they will make sense. Another aspect of the world, formerly unknown, is now part of the universe she knows and understands. Every time an aspect of the unexplored territory is processed successfully, we get more rules, more wisdom, more distinctions, we advance our map. We benefit from so doing. We experience more mastery and are rewarded with feelings of stability and self-confidence.

Initially the unexplored domain is chaos and confusion. Later, once explored, we grasp the intrinsic order that initially eluded us. "Oh. Now I get it." It turns out that chaos usually has a potential for order that we can extract or create. We do so and now we've learned a few things. Our map is now more sophisticated; we can do more, move forward in ways we earlier could not.

The mystical perspective upholds Peterson's understanding of chaos and order but with one premise: If the world as we know it is comprised of Divinity, then there necessarily is the most exquisite order at the root of creation. But because G-d cloaks himself, his filters disguise the inner order and create the possibility for the existence of evil. A chaotic veneer then masks the intrinsic order. If we burrow deep enough, we can crack the code, find that order and reveal that which was concealed but present all along. One way we see this play out is when people respond to catastrophe triumphant, having cultivated greater faith, depth, gratitude, awareness or accrued other gains. Some undergo terrible trials and conclude that the event was life-changing . . . for the good. That dark night of the soul, for some, is a path to Divinity. Joseph Campbell said, "Where you stumble and fall, there you find gold." More on that later.

In all chaos, there is a cosmos. In all disorder, a secret order.
Carl Jung

Is it Chaos or Our Own Immaturity?

Let's look at the developmental process just mentioned. Think, as above, a baby perceiving a household, a family, the sights and sounds of home life, as chaotic. It's not really chaotic, though. The baby's perceptual apparatus is undeveloped so the world appears chaotic. Similarly, when we see chaos, we are initially oblivious to the Divinity that underpins every facet of the world. Maybe with spiritual growth the individual will, in retrospect, say that that illness was the best thing that ever happened. If that occurs, the person who now perceives the crisis as an opportunity is equivalent to the baby whose perceptual acuity have improved, allowing for a more positive and less traumatized experience of normal family processes. Chaos gives way to order.

That not withstanding, it can take years to find the silver-lining in a negative event. And sometimes malevolence is so untoward it is frankly impossible to find it. Peterson's insight that we experience aspects of the world with which we are unfamiliar as unsettling and disorienting, stands. We live our lives confronting what seems like chaos, foraging and ultimately, hopefully, expanding our maps en route to gaining a richer and fuller relationship with and understanding of the Divinity at the core of creation.

The Hero's Journey

As that process of development unfolds, as we move further afield and explore the unknown, we are undertaking the hero's journey. In Genesis, 12, 1, the text reads, "G-d said to Abram, 'Go for yourself from your land, from your relatives, and from your father's house to the land I will show you.' This command sanctions moving away from the familiar into the unknown, for all humanity, forevermore. We walk in Abraham's footsteps with each step forward, providing, of course, the movement is in a sanctioned direction ("the land I will show you") and not a stroll in no man's land![2] Don't just catapult yourself to any G-d forsaken place! We are meant to follow the paths outlined in tried and true sacred traditions. Premised here, then, is the necessity of a relationship with the G-d ideal, something Peterson points out is lacking in secular society, but that will be discussed later.

So – to review – we are constantly meant to thrust forward. At any given time there are aspects of the world which we completely understand and other aspects that are a complete mystery and our task is to continue to approach and discover new terrain. As a kid, you learn to ride a bike. At age 16, it might be time for driving lessons. Bike riding has become old hat, as the saying goes, but the rules of the road as a driver of a car – that's unexplored territory – until you master it. You take your lessons, get some practice. That formerly unexplored territory is now explored. The next challenge awaits you, around the corner. And so on, and so forth. Get your bearings, build your map, and you are equipping yourself with what you need to undertake your Hero's journey!

The nature of the Divinity on earth is to be hidden, but you can deploy your own Divinity to motor an ongoing effort to perfect your innate deficiencies. You do this by seeking out contact with aspects of Divinity that are hidden from your lineage. We assume your parents and family have been bringing forward a degree of order/Divinity, their life work. But stepping to the plate means you have to move beyond what they did. We trust you integrated what they had to give you and teach when you grew up at their address. Now you must leave home in order to uncover other aspects of Divinity, to break new ground, learning new disciplines, meeting new people (each of whom are, like you, expressions of Divinity), and so undertaking the Hero's journey.

Lest we assume that the unexplored dimension only relates to that which is outside of us, bear in mind that even our own bodies can trip us into an experience of the unexplored. Perhaps a person becomes sick and their body does not work as it did. These changes throw us into confusion and chaos. Even the removal of a tooth, Peterson reflects, will have us excavating the interior of the mouth with the tongue, potentially for months, as we recalibrate to the mouth that has become unfamiliar given the change of the interior landscape. Eventually the new circumstance becomes the new normal. We move from unknown to known, chaos to order.

When you live with your body in its usual familiar state, you are dealing with the mirage of the physical world. The body has its place in the world of things; it functions in the familiar way. You feel that you can count on it, that it has a degree of solidity and stability. It is mostly invisible to you when it feels fine. You feel like you are living in the world of things, with a physical reality, a body, that has its own stable, ongoing function that you can rely on.

Then there is a health crisis. It becomes clear that there was nothing reliable and solid about the body, which, now changed, is painful or a cause of worry. We have been catapulted out of the mirage to a very different and more realistic awareness. In those moments, we confront mortality and, arguably, encounter Divinity. If the situation abates, leaving a change in the day-to-day experience of the body, there is this re-acclimation process. In Peterson's language, you are recalibrating and creating a new order, getting used to new, changed circumstances. Then you can get back to treating your body like it's a static thing in a world of things that stay relatively static. Or you may be integrating lessons that relate to Divinity: holding an awareness that your recuperation is an act of grace; that current medical advances are truly the stuff of miracles; that the body is on an inevitable decline leading to humility, frustration or fear, all inviting more thoughtful contemplation of the limits of life and inviting a change of priorities. So, as in the case mentioned above, while the body recalibrates to change, the soul, too, may undertake its own process of redefining understandings.

And this is life. There is an infinite domain of realities, experiences, disciplines, etc.. The older we get, the more learnings and experience we accrue, the realm of the explored expands, the realm of the unexplored shrinks, the map gets more detailed and sophisticated; hopefully this process continues to our very last day, enhancing our competence, generating yet more wisdom. Still, some aspects of the unexplored territory will always remain unexplored. How can we understand some of the enigmas and paradoxes that science reveals but cannot explain? What happens after death? Is there a spiritual infrastructure to this world, something that we cannot see? Ultimately the unexplored territory takes us to the heart of mystery.

All of which, that which we can fathom and that which we will never fathom, being the address of G-d.

The 'Unknown Unknown'

Once we understand the concept of the unknown, Peterson introduces an additional concept: the "unknown unknown." Say you have a plan to study radiography. You begin your studies and while the topic has you dabbling in unknown territory, you have undertaken this study voluntarily and the process of learning is orderly. You are navigating the 'known unknown' towards the end of extending the dimension of reality you know to include radiography.

In sharp contrast, there are times we are hurtled into 'unknown territory' under duress, forced by unforeseen circumstances that occur suddenly. We call these events disasters or emergencies; also, the proverbial dark night of the soul. Whether it be a medical diagnosis, falling victim to a crime or accident or being betrayed by someone we thought we knew, the individual descends into chaos. The individual's world becomes foreign and unfamiliar. All bearings are lost. There is a greater level of strain associated with the "unknown unknown," potentially resulting in post-traumatic stress or a general depletion of resources (physical, emotional, financial, etc). The possibility of experiencing the 'unknown unknown' is always near at hand, a source of anxiety for the timid. Fearing unforeseen negative outcomes, some may defensively avoid the unknown dimension at all costs. Peterson also points out that because we can imagine our own death that fear can contaminate the realm of the unknown. "What if dabbling with the unexplored leads to death?" This fear conjures up additional worries regarding the unknown.

Peterson often quotes a line from Proverbs, the first 'prayer' said by observant Jews when they arise in the morning: "The beginning of wisdom is the fear of G-d." I've heard Dennis Prager discuss a premise of Judaism: If you fear G-d, prompting your priority to behave in moral ways and uphold appropriate rules, you will not fear death, disaster, rejection or any other event or outcome which people normally fear. The idea is we rightly have a certain amount of fear which we will experience in life, but if we direct the fear appropriately we will behave in a way that leaves us little to fear!

Ultimately, since the religious premise is that everything IS G-d, when we harbor fears, we are effectively fearing His unknown ways. In secular society, there is no active concept of G-d introduced to children. They will therefore lack an outlet for their fear and then children may suffer a more generalized experience of anxiety which makes it difficult for them to animate the Hero archetype.

Life involves taking action and there are so many good reasons for feeling unsure about how to move forward. The physical world provides context but fails to provide clear directions. You see a given physical reality and you may be uncertain: how to birth what 'is' into a better outcome? And which outcome to pursue? Then: how to achieve the goal? How to make a new friend? How to resolve a health problem? Every day involves countless choices. What to eat? How to cook it? And considering your next move, there may be associated risks – the "unknown unknown" lurks in the background. What if you don't have all the information you need to prevent a misstep? So much of the terrain is unexplored. You could take a decisive action and face negative consequences you did not foresee.

Fortunately, we are outfitted with two parts of the brain, each of which is specialized to deal with one or the other aspect of reality, the known or the unknown. Together, we use them to cobble together a map of life, a task that we start in childhood, but continue doing throughout our lives. The right and left hemispheres are the tools we bring to the task of decoding reality; they allow us to face the unknown and build the map of meaning.

In Genesis, we learn that the human is made in the image of the Divine, "masculine and feminine, he created them." (Genesis 1:27). G-d provides these two parts of the mind, "the masculine and the feminine' to help us cope with challenges, the perfect equipment that we can use to find Him, hidden as he is in our world. We have to use them properly, in the right sequence, deploying the right choreography, so to speak, to be in our 'right mind'.

Right and Left Brain

Peterson talks extensively about how the two hemispheres work in tandem to help us orient to reality. He cites the work of Neuroscientist Elkhonon Goldberg who posits that the right brain and the left brain have specific roles to play, relative to the known and unknown dimensions of reality. The right brain orients to the realm of novelty, the unknown dimension. It takes a quick look at new situations/environments, surveying for patterns that are familiar. It's as if we take a picture of the big picture to see if any part reminds us of some other context that we have experienced or mastered.

You hear a sudden loud noise. You freeze. You scan the environment. Then, wordlessly you get your bearings, drawing upon past life experience which provides the only frame of reference you could possibly have. Finally the nonverbal right brain comprehends what's happening, where this noise came from and what it means. Next the left brain gears up, and puts words to the right brain's hunch. Using logic and analysis, the left brain provides a detailed sequence of directions or thoughts, allowing you to respond to your situation. "Close the window." "Call the police."

Let's say that you're in the kitchen doing a few simple kitchen chores. Suddenly, you notice sharp stinging pain in your eyes. You freeze in a state of vigilant awareness. You experience a pang of anxiety. That's the right brain's response when adjusting to novel circumstances. The negativity alerts you to stop everything and survey the situation. The right brain, faced with a sudden anomaly, surveys the scene, trying to detect a pattern. Memory flashes. The left brain then verbalizes what the right brain came up with: "oh, right. Cutting onions irritates the eyes!" Right brain has silently surveyed the context, searching for and finding stored learnings which generate the insight: "No emergency! This is a familiar pattern!" Now left brain articulates what's going on and triggers the details, thoughts about what I can do about this: "Turn on the kitchen fan." "Leave the room."

To summarize: the right brain registers negative affect, triggers a shut down of action and moves into a mode of vigilant observation. It perceives the *gestalt* of a situation, looking, metaphorically speaking, with a flood light at the big picture. It strives to clarify a situation or context, then hands the insight to the left brain which can put words to it. The left brain, the filing cabinet, stores details about any given aspect of reality. “How to cook vegetable soup? Here are the steps.”

So we have these two parts of the mind, each of which specializes in helping us process either the known or unknown dimensions of reality. It is more comfortable dealing with the known dimension, of course. There is more predictability dealing with the known. The unknown, at least initially, may induce confusion, frustration or even overwhelm. But it also awakens our curiosity and facilitates mastery when we ultimately comprehend and manage that which initially confounded us.

Imagine you were a mystic from yesteryear and you were trying to determine the task of humanity. “What are we here to do?” You pick up the Hebrew Bible and start reading. Every time you read the word ‘good’, you get excited. The sun, the moon . . . Good! Each good means that humanity is not here to improve on that creation. It’s good enough! No need to make a better sun or moon. Animals . . . all good! Plant life. . . Good! Finally you come upon “not good.” This is it! This must be the job of humanity!

What is it? Having created Adam, G-d reflects, “it is not good for man to be alone.” So curious. If it’s not good for man to be alone, why doesn’t the comment come from man himself? The answer: Masculine consciousness does not know that it’s not good for it to be alone. Let’s focus on the intra-psychic dimension of life right now. There are two parts of self. The conscious self, the inner Yang, thinks that it’s the boss. After all, its job is to negotiate the world ‘out there’. With regards to the unconscious (the Yin self), the conscious thinks that that part of the self, which knows the inner terrain and tosses up a dream now and then, is an after thought, irrelevant, unnecessary. The conscious self does not know that it is not good for it to be alone!

Time and time again we will see breakthrough when the two aspects of self work in tandem with each other, with a proper choreography. One manifestation of this is the elegant back and forth function of the right brain and the left brain. That's what we are talking about here. In fact, virtually any bodily process involves the choreography of Yin and Yang. Breathing, the beat of the heart, peristalsis, the movement of the eye which alternates from focus to periphery vision, back and forth, back and forth. The structure of our duality is the signature of our Divinity. "Male and Female, He created them." The art of life is to deploy these faculties in a way that is synchronized and effective. Left to our own devices, that doesn't always happen, unless we implement the right processes.

Peterson suggests the healthiest, most stable, most satisfied individuals, those who find greatest meaning in life, are those "who live on the edge of what they know;" on one hand, anchored in the zone of the familiar which provides stability, but dabbling with that which is new and unfamiliar, and subsequently energized by new thoughts and experiences. For Peterson, the person who rightly traverses the known and unknown dimensions of reality in a balanced way recreates paradise on earth "so that the forces of the cosmos are properly balanced in one's being and all feels right in the world."

This is the definition of mental health, then, and these are people who we enjoy spending time with. They are animating both aspects, the masculine and the feminine. They shine light!

The Stick in the Mud

Some people, though, insist on sticking with the familiar, avoiding the unexplored realm. "I just want to rely on what I know and leave it at that!" Bad plan. For one thing, there will be mental health ramifications. It could look like obsessive-compulsive disorder; somebody who overly fixates on the details and fails to activate the holistic pattern detecting right brain. The result is rigidity. A lack of wisdom. A person prone to repetition in thought and speech; the type who others experience as 'boring' and 'repetitive'; Someone who fixates on minutia; Someone necessarily prone to anxiety, further fueling the drive to avoid anything unfamiliar.

Left brain is dominant. Right brain, un-landscaped, under-utilized.

Such a person quickly falls behind the times. Peterson gives the example of electronics which constantly need to be updated as current operating software becomes out of date. Peterson cites Alice in Wonderland; the Red Queen tells Alice, "in my kingdom, you have to run as fast as you can to stay in place." For Peterson, that quote represents the need to access aspects of the unknown just to keep up with everyone and everything else. After all, there are always new processes, new technologies, new visions, new mentalities coming down the pike. Keep your head in the sand and you become irrelevant. No wonder we tell seniors to learn a new language or take up a new sport. Dabbling with the unfamiliar keeps us fresh, vital, interested and interesting. Otherwise we stagnate.

"Wonder, not doubt, is the beginning of knowledge."
A. J. Heschel

The truth is even if you firmly resolved to only engage with that which you know, it wouldn't work. Anytime you try to achieve something, if it works the way you thought it would, you are in known territory. You get it. You achieved the outcome you were trying for, are satisfied, and ready to move on to your next goal. The problem is any number of times in life you try to achieve a particular outcome using the best of what you know to achieve success and. . . Damn! It didn't work!

Turns out your map was slightly off, given some variable you hadn't accommodated. You have hit a wall, entered the zone of the unknown. "Why didn't that work?" Using the right brain, you have to redouble your efforts and revisit what is now clearly unexplored terrain to figure out what you did wrong and how to get it right. You are like the GPS – "recalibrating, recalibrating."

Hopefully you figure it out, modify your behavior and get your desired result. If you do, you have extended the explored terrain. Moving forward you will make more distinctions, ones you weren't aware of before, when navigating the same territory. You will feel more competent, experience a greater sense of security and stability.

So clearly even if you intend on never dabbling with the unknown, it's still going to find you! Wrestle with it, crack it open and pull out the understandings that had eluded you and you will grow. Walk away discouraged and resentful and you may become chronically bitter. More on that later.

This is the stuff of life. Or the way Peterson puts it: when we engage with the unknown we gather more information and in so doing we get further "formed." He says 'InFORMation' helps us to form ourselves! We don't just retool, we literally "reconstitute" ourselves. In other words, contact with the unknown strengthens and builds our core identities. It changes who we are. And every day provides more opportunity to reach into another bit of unknown territory and thereby expand our map . . . and ourselves.

And our relationship to Divinity. Every field of knowledge is another expression of Divinity and the more we explore, the more we revivify ourselves with the glory of His ways, with the bounty of His knowledge, with the genius embedded within creation. The more we do that, the more we unpack our own Divinity, the more we learn about the various expressions and permutations of Divinity, the more meaning we discover in life. G-d is truly the life of this party!

The Resistant Among Us

The more advantageous posture, we said, is to dabble with the unknown, in bite size increments. If some avoid the realm of the unexplored territory, others take it a step further. Consider a person who assumes a posture of certainty, the confident type who effectively asserts: "Everything I know is what I need to know. I don't need to know anything beyond that." Peterson characterizes this posture as pathological stultification. This individual is unwilling to explore new vistas.

In Peterson's mind, this person has made an alliance with the devil. They will prioritize their own personal interest. Peterson says their lives are a living hell. They will have a low tolerance for anything out of the ordinary and will react with heightened aggression when confronted with anything that challenges their vision, their politic, their status quo. They will be prone to paranoia, fixated on maintaining security (control) and seeing threat everywhere.

Why can they trust no one; not even life itself? People who can trust their own ability to delve into unknown territory experience resilience. They perceive themselves as strong and able. These people trust themselves and thus they can trust others and even life, itself. People who recoil from the unknown feel vulnerable and suspicious. They cannot trust.

The Map You Need

It becomes clear that not only do we need a map that will help us navigate both the unexplored and the explored terrain but, ideally, we need a map that strongly encourages us to explore both of these terrains, and each in the right way, at the right and appropriate moment. Avoiding the unexplored leads to rigidity but pursuing that domain excessively or prematurely can be detrimental, as well. Maybe a young person who delves into new areas – sexual experience, religious observance, esoteric knowledge – without adequate grounding, maturity or readiness, may find any of these realms to be over-stimulating and disorganizing. Too much of the unexplored terrain experienced too early or too intensely, wreaks havoc. Perhaps that's why we have the expression, "when the student is ready, the teacher appears." That saying could express a hope more than a fact!

As we go along, we realize that we need to move forward in deliberate measured ways, we must cultivate a map which will guide our efforts for the duration of a lifetime, and, since we don't come with operating instructions, putting together an accurate map is going to be a DIY project.

That's why we need sacred traditions! This task should not be a DIY project. When I was a teen, I followed the teen idols of the day. One family, The Osmond's, were well known, a group of brothers and a sister. The Osmond's were committed Mormons. Another family group, The Jackson 5, were also popular during the same years.

I've been thinking about the Osmond's of late because the siblings, now in their sixties, are coming through the YouTube feed. Their children and grandchildren have assembled videos, a montage of family photos documenting the legacy of long-standing marriages. What is the secret sauce that has former teen idol Donny Osmond enjoying his grandchildren while superstar Michael Jackson, formerly of the Jackson 5, is dead, felled years ago by a drug overdose? Donny Osmond had a better map! And he didn't have to make it, through, trial and error, by himself. He benefitted from a heritage that could inform him.

Culture to the Rescue!

Society is comprised of people, each of whom has to navigate a reality full of ambiguity – not only because of the unexplored territory. Ambiguity is also a product of life being dynamic. There are many changing circumstances to navigate in any given day. Each individual has different talents and weaknesses and he or she will need to manage and express them while also competently getting along with others and juggling different roles and circumstances. Each person must express and also regulate the self, while navigating whatever comes up. A good map will be key and that map better be available to us starting at a young age.

Damn. It's not.

So culture helps us out. Firstly, culture establishes a social order, creating norms and structures that help people live together in an organized way. Culture, therefore, advances its own map which guides interactions between people and establishes norms about how to relate in different contexts. True, these structures, implemented excessively can become tyrannical and oppressive. Despite that risk, the benefits have members of society living in harmony with each other. When citizens abide by the cultural norms and rules, they experience stability and avoid lives characterized by chaos and uncertainty.

Secondly, culture embeds specific knowledge, teaching implicit lessons that can help children understand the world while accessing ancestral wisdom that has accumulated over the generations. All this wisdom can be relayed in myth, in the language of the arts, in nursery rhymes.

Why through these mediums? We have already learned that the right brain is the portal of entry for learning about the unexplored dimension. If you wish to introduce new ideas, and if you want those ideas to stick, you best introduce them using the medium that specifically targets the right brain. The right brain activates with metaphor and story, imagination and emotion. The right brain processes myths and fables. Peterson frequently deconstructs iconic myths and stories, showing the embedded lessons that are relayed in the story and in the symbols within, hidden meanings which are lapped up by the right brain of the young child. Peterson demonstrates, in his fascinating writings and lectures, how society uses culture to help young people cultivate a working map that will help them learn how to live well amongst others and otherwise how to conduct themselves.

"Genuine poetry can communicate before it is understood."
T.S. Eliot

Deconstructing Little Red Riding Hood

Let's look at one simple example that I draw from my frame of reference. Remember the children's story, *Little Red Riding Hood*? This little girl dressed in a red cape wanders through the forest to visit her grandmother. When she finally gets to grandmother's house she sees that Granny's facial patterns resemble those of a wolf. Indeed, the wolf has dressed in Granny's clothing.

Little Red Riding Hood undertakes a process. She doesn't just throw herself into interaction with Granny. She pauses, experiencing the hesitation typical of the right brain in the face of novel stimuli. Then she undergoes the pattern detection process associated with the right brain. Compare: Granny's eyes to these eyes. Granny's ears to these ears. Hmmm. In the end, the little girl correctly identifies that this is not her grandmother, first by activating her right brain, then, her left brain.

On first glance, we see a story that teaches the child that situations exist in which the normal explored terrain, visiting Granny, gives way, unexpectedly, to unexplored terrain. The story provides a lesson how the child can manage anomalous events, many of which will likely occur over the span of the child's lifetime. The story teaches children how to engage the right brain process of pattern detection to understand and manage unfamiliar situations. But is there more embedded in this tale?

Now if we deconstruct the message, think about the following. The color red associates, say, with the stop sign or a red traffic light. Stop! Sometimes red is an indicator of danger. According to one source, the wolf is a symbol representing the threat of rape.[3]

Interesting. Now we have a story that cloaks a little girl in red, the color that warns of danger. And while she's intending to meet her Granny, someone vitally concerned for her well being, she discerns that she is dealing with a predator, all this by doing a right brain analysis of the anomaly.

Could this be a metaphor? She properly identifies the wolf because she has cloaked herself in the red cape, representing a cautious outlook which trips her into the analysis that gets her to the right answer. We see a message embedded by culture for little girls who, many years later, will be navigating the world of boys! The culture quietly seeds the knowledge that there may be wolves who otherwise assume the guise of Granny. And culture communicates this teaching in a way that will not be detected by the child's conscious mind. How's that for implicit learning?

So many times, parents, culture has your back. Classic literature, fairytales, creative productions that have attracted widespread interest, often are carriers of important cultural messages. If Humpty Dumpty is so pervasive that it's known by three-year-olds as well as 90-year-olds, expect to find an important message embedded within it! Having said that, we also need to point out that any number of times there can be cultural productions which embed counterproductive teachings. An upcoming chapter addresses this. The point here is not to imply that every cultural message is productive. It is good to know, though, that some classic narratives communicate implicit truths given that each person has to come up with their own map of meaning and we can use whatever help we can access, in order to do so.

Sacred Traditions to the Rescue

And the best help of all comes from sacred traditions. I wrote my original summary for a secular audience and within it I describe my understanding of Peterson's message. But I wouldn't bank on the idea that a media diet of Disney hits relays the most inspired metaphors that will help kids grow into moral beings. There is no reason to expect a secular culture will properly promote the psycho-spiritual growth of young people. Sometimes it does. Other times, not. Given many cultural productions that deliver empty calories, so to speak, don't be surprised that we have people falling into pseudo-religions, aligning with extreme ideologies, engaging in celebrity worship or finding other non-ideal replacements for religion and the G-d ideal.

Indeed, Peterson correctly identifies important messages embedded in many classic iconic fables. He also understands, though, that the priority of science as a lens has created a disinterest in the myths and cultural narratives from sacred traditions that, historically, helped children integrate important messages and so shaped their maps of meaning. This leads to a discussion of why those who grow up in a secular culture are effectively disadvantaged, when it comes to the map of meaning.

What's Wrong with the Societal Map of Meaning?

We've agreed that culture can, at times, help socialize children by embedding positive values within myths or cultural narratives. But society and culture also sometimes perpetuate negative ideas that we similarly internalize. Let's look at one important example: in contemporary life, science and technology is currently perceived as the language of progress and has become the lens through which we prefer to view our lives and make decisions. Recall that Peterson asserts we are hardwired to learn values and life lessons via the right brain which interprets the unknown and unfamiliar aspects of the world through myths and narratives. He suggests that we best learn how to behave by watching the hero and learn how not to behave by watching the villain. In a society that emphasizes scientific knowledge, though, there is less emphasis on those right brain modalities that he claims most effectively teach how to be a cooperative citizen.

Further and most importantly, Peterson insists the ultimate venue for relating these value laden stories is in the context of a religious tradition. Narratives can present a religious worldview that relays spiritual teachings. For thousands of years, religion was central to most civilizations and only receded in importance with the dawning of the scientific age. Now rationalism discourages us away from 'fairytales' that were guiding narratives in other eras.

Richard Rohr conjectures that yesteryear's myths have been replaced with "disorienting narratives like communism, fascism, terrorism, mass production, and its counterpart, consumerism." (Rohr, 2010, Introduction)

He's right. Our current narratives *are* disorienting. And, for that matter, modern day heroes are often revealed or conjectured to be exactly the opposite, all of which serves to trash the standing of the hero archetype, more generally. Narratives from yesteryear, on the other hand, with clearly articulated heroes and villains, created cohesion. People could share a worldview and cooperate, informed by and working within the same value system. In fact, the hardiness of those old-time narratives, which took root in the implicit nondeclarative memory of the earlier generation, is that they continue to influence today's secular society. You could say the religiosity of yesteryear continues to 'off gas', registering as a form of implicit knowledge, although its influence and hold on us gets weaker with time.

"Science takes things apart to see how they work. Religion puts things together to see what they mean."
Rabbi Jonathan Sacks

We've heard the idea 'a fish does not know the water it swims in.' Similarly, we each are steeped in the mentality that characterizes our day and age. We don't realize how we think, what we think, that so many of our premises are a function of the worldview that preceded ours; a worldview that revered divinity and viewed a relationship with the Divine as an essential part of life. Contemporary interest in religion has faded, but we, none the less, bear a faint though discernible influence of our devout ancestors, harboring implicit knowledge that tells us that doing the right and good thing is important, a notion that emanates more rightly from an earlier era than from our own. In other words, thousands of years of religiosity continues to influence our thinking.

One sign of that influence is a norm whereby people agree that some behaviors are immoral; that there is such a thing as morality. And a secular person may very well argue that his or her sense of morality exists independent of any premise about the existence of a universal god. Yet, from a philosophical point of view, it is hard to defend any particular system of morality as absolutely true and necessarily binding, since one society might have values which differ from another. Some societies might hold that undergoing female genital mutilation is a worthy rite of passage in a particular spiritual system. Without one absolute source that defines what constitutes moral or immoral behavior, there's really no case to be made that one culture's practices are sacred while another's are barbaric.

Peterson asserts that it is only the premise that humans are made in the image of the Divine that obligates us to revere every human life. That value only wields authority because of the authority from which it came. Today we find ourselves in an era where people have an ethical sensibility as an implicit felt sense but without a relationship to organized religion that inculcates us with higher level teachings, our morality is predicated on the crumbs of our ancestors' piety. We will not be able to perpetuate these values in the generations that come, so weak is our hold on and grasp of the moral sensibility. In other words, we are on our way down, not up.

At Least This . . .

To review, according to Peterson the religious framework of yesteryear infuses us, permeating our frames of reference on an ethereal level so that it plays a role in our thinking in some sort of hazy way, telling us what we are like, who we are meant to be, what standard we are to live up to. You might think of the attitudes and mentalities of our ancestors serving as a platform on which rests our more modern conceptualization of the world. Their sensibilities are our floorboards. We don't notice them, but they hold us up, at least for now.[4]

How do we see the influence of the religious sensibility as it infuses the secular mentality? If I can introduce some of my own reading at this point, Ann Coulter, author of, *Godless: The Church of Liberalism*, suggests that moderns can discharge the religious impulse of yesteryear by participating in ideologies that serve as substitute religions. She suggests that old-style religion dictates religious rituals whereas the new religion prescribes its own rituals: vegetarianism, recycling, organic gardening, etc. The religions of yesteryear advocated chastity in adolescence and ensconced sexuality as a fixture in marriage only. The new religion construes that teaching children all the permutations of sexual expression is virtuous and normalizes sexuality outside of marriage.

In the religion of yesteryear, members of the clergy perpetuate the tradition by teaching and lecturing. In this new era, Coulter suggests, the high school teachers are the purveyors of the tradition, teaching contemporary ideologies – gender differences are solely a product of nurture, not nature, as one example – always in a school where the Lord's prayer is banned. Coulter holds that the testament of the new religion is 'Roe vs Wade' and its sacrament is abortion. In other words, though the beliefs of the liberal sensibility stand in direct contrast to those at the core of the Judeo-Christian tradition, the fact that there is a priority to uphold values and live in a structure that mimics that of organized religion reflects the imprint of our pious forbearers.

Let's look at another example. Kathryn Lofton, Assistant Professor of Religious Studies at Yale University, points out that fandom of celebrities is another modern day pseudo-religion. In her book, *Oprah: The Gospel of an Icon*, she also suggests that Oprah and her plethora of products function as a substitute religion. She writes,

> [Oprah] preaches prosperity gospel, she advocates books as scripture, she offers exegesis, she conducts exculpatory rights, she supplies a bazaar of faithful practices, she propagates missions, both home and foreign. She opines repeatedly on the meaning of existence, the seat of the soul, the purpose of your life, and the place of a higher calling. Oprah plays religious even as she is, most adamantly (by scholarly classification and by her own), not a religion (Lofton, 2011, p. 9).

Peterson would say that, running on fumes, we have an appetite for ideologies or structures that mimic religion and take us back to old time values. I wonder if that's what motivates constant remakes of old movies, TV series, shows that have younger performers singing the hits of superstars of yesterday. Something compels us to turn back time in a society that otherwise venerates the new and improved. Likely our ancestors spent time each week looking to the root of creation, thinking about who they find there and considering the ramifications for their lives. In contrast, we binge watch old TV series and watch remakes of old movies.

If Peterson, and Nietzsche are right, we are subject to a sensibility that is fading out and once it fades out once and for all, another will emerge, likely one completely divorced from the sensibility of religion. Or religions themselves get corrupted, as suggested by Rohr. He notes that when we abandon healing myths we get "trapped" in destructive myths. [5] Which ever way it goes, it takes us closer to the dissolution of our civilization. Peterson thinks we are gradually floating away from the roots of our civility.

According to Peterson, once we have detached ourselves from a core source of knowledge, the religions that used to inform a level of inner knowledge that is more ephemeral and less articulated, we risk losing our bearings. We will simply come to believe wrong things or attach ourselves to wrong ideas, falling into a sickness of spirit. The only cure, he says, is to integrate a system of belief and representation which will organize the structure of our thoughts. If we don't have a coherent system of belief and representation, we will succumb to disastrous ideologies. Peterson describes these ideologies as "crippled religions . . . like religions but it's missing an arm and a leg… It hobbles along… It gives you some security in terms of group identification but ultimately it is a parasite living on something pure and true."

Another way Peterson expresses it: "when we knock out the slats out of the base of western civilization by destroying this representation – this G-d ideal – we oscillate, moving to the extremes of nihilism and radical or extreme ideologies" Harboring knowledge and information without that ideal providing a solid base potentially throws us off. The more latent and subtle level of knowing becomes weak, disconnected from higher truths that provide stability. We become dissociated from truth and from our deeper selves. And we fall for the bait: the idea that we can create religions to suit our desires, imagining these self-constructed systems will help us weather the challenges that life presents.

Peterson invites us to find our way back to some form of reverence. He certainly does not advocate any particular religious path. Each can find their own. But he shares works from the various world religions, teaching the wisdom embedded within and hopefully rattling chains so that his readers and listeners will continue reading and learning, all the while wrangling with the ideas that can inform the personal map and help access meaning.

Peterson has dedicated himself to the task of helping a whole generation reconnect with core implicit knowledge, providing bearings that allow a person to better construct a healthy map of reality. He has taken on the fight against a pervading dominant sensibility, armed primarily with classic ideas that people can use to repopulate the inner dimension of knowing.

"The creative artist and poet and saint must fight the actual (as opposed to the ideal) gods of our society – the god of conformism as well as the gods of apathy, material success, and exploitive power. These are the "idols" of our society that are worshiped by multitudes of people."

Rollo May

This book is a call to arms. The sacred traditions are needed now more than ever to bring forward ancient maps that can help young people who are questing to move forward in meaningful ways. In the next chapter, I'd like to take a deeper dive into the duality of mind so we can see why, as Peterson states, the G-d ideal is unequivocally helpful for those trying to make sense of the (seeming) chaos in our world while simultaneously working to sort themselves out.

Notes

1. Sarah Schneider summarizes this part of the creation process in Chapter 5 of her book, Kabbalistic Writings in the Nature of Masculine & Feminine. I cannot recommend this fascinating book strongly enough, for anyone interested in this topic or the topic of that book.
2. Peterson is quoted as saying, "As you wander off the path, the probability that you will wander further off the path increases non-linearly."
3. Rabbi Yitzchak Ginsburgh has discussed this in his writings
4. Peterson reflects, "We live on the corpse of our culture . . . but the system has to be revivified." We live in a secular society that has people abandoning religion. The system is not being revivified. Without bona fide religion actively suffusing it, it will fizzle out for good.
5. Seems to me, one example could be the Jihad's understanding that the reward for killing the enemy is access to 72 virgins in Heaven.

2.

Architecting the Mind: "What's G-d Got to Do with It?"

The pen moved slowly and awkwardly. The young woman seemed unaware that she was writing. Psychiatrist Milton Erickson, a pioneer in the use of clinical hypnosis, was demonstrating his technique to the class. The students were quietly observing what was clearly an altered state of consciousness. Afterwards, a woman approached the doctor. In the past weeks, she had been doodling, defacing table cloths at restaurants or writing in her notebook, all without awareness. She wondered: could hypnosis reveal the meaning of her doodles or help relieve her anxiety?[1]

Erickson agreed to see her. At a meeting, she described herself as the only child of parents who adored her. Her home life was happy; Her entry to college, uneventful. Regarding personal problems, she could only think of one. Her friendship with 'Jane' had withered over time. The growing emotional distance left 'Ann', we will call her, feeling lonely and resentful. In her mind, though, this situation had nothing to do with her symptoms.

As she spoke, she mindlessly picked up a pencil and doodled lines and shapes. Only at the close of the interview did she become aware of doodling.

At that meeting, Erickson made several hypnotic suggestions: the unconscious was to organize the material and decide on a tangible way that it would communicate with her. She was to keep busy until the next appointment, giving no conscious thought to her troubles. At the next appointment, she was to avoid mention of her symptoms and concerns.

The next day Ann felt so well, she almost chose not to attend the session. She did come, though, deciding to give an account of the book she was reading. She sat beside a desk with Erickson across from her. This arrangement allowed her to pick up a pencil and mindlessly doodle while focusing on Erickson.

As she discussed the book, she began drawing absentmindedly. She drew lines and shapes and squiggles, then a second drawing where she seemed to be rearranging the lines and shapes she had randomly drawn earlier, this time constructing a picture. There was a cylinder, a large triangle and a small triangle, all within a square. These shapes were connected to each other. Then there was a squiggly line seemingly emitted from the cylinder which traversed past the boundary of the square and connected to the top of a triangle outside the square. Once she completed that drawing, she glanced at it quickly, seemingly unaware of what she had drawn.

Erickson gave her an opportunity to communicate about the drawing, telling her that the unconscious mind could make a vertical line to indicate 'yes' or a horizontal line to indicate 'no'. He asked her, "is it all there?" She replied, "I suppose so, if there is anything there at all." Her hand, without her awareness, moved vertically to indicate 'yes'. She described the urge to give something to Erickson, something that seemed relevant though she did not know why, and then handed the doctor a packet of matches which advertised a local hotel.

She then looked at her watch, seemed anxious to leave, but was willing to comment on the drawing. She hypothesized that the cylinder and the squiggly line coming out of it was a cigarette with smoke. Everybody in her family smoked. Perhaps, she reflected, the matches belonged to her father. Erickson told her to call when she was ready to know a bit more. She left quickly.

She had two more meetings with Erickson over the next weeks. She said she was ‘getting ready to know something she already knows’. She also made a date with Jane to whom she was harboring terrible ill will. Jane refused to identify her boyfriend, fearing Ann would know him. Ann was oddly jealous, as if this boyfriend was her own . . . except Ann did not have a boyfriend! She predicted a fight with Jane at that meeting and a fight with her father that same night, although she couldn’t imagine why.

That evening she fought with Jane. And with her father. She screamed at him: “I wasn’t born yesterday” and “I know what this is all about.” The next day, she told Erickson this outburst made no sense. Now, ready to understand the drawing, she asked Erickson for a “starting word” to spur her awareness. Erickson said, “Some time ago, you told me you were terribly interested in and fascinated by symbolism.” He also pulled the matches from the hotel and dropped them on the table. (Erickson & Kubie in Wedding & Corsini, 1979), p. 290).

Ann burst into tears, now realizing that Jane and her father were romantically involved, regularly meeting at the hotel named on the matches. Erickson’s comment on symbolism had prompted her thought that, for Freud, a cylinder represented the phallus. The connection between the cylinder and the external triangle represented father’s affair with Jane.

When confronted, Jane confirmed the relationship, also revealing the father’s long history of affairs. Ann’s priority was that the relationship be hidden from her mother. Jane agreed. Now, with the matter settled, Ann’s anxiety completely lifted! The doodling stopped. Ann stayed in touch with Erickson, went on to get married. The symptoms never returned.

This case introduces us to a part of the mind that we all have, though rarely experience in quite so dramatic a way. Looking at the adaptive unconscious, though, is our inroad to Peterson’s insights about Divinity. We must start here.

The Adaptive Unconscious

This chapter further explores the non-verbal unconscious faculty that we possess which helps us register and adapt to reality. In the last chapter's discussion of the right brain, we merely touched the surface, citing a part which activates in the face of the unknown to orient a person. Erickson's case more richly demonstrates that faculty which harbors information out of conscious awareness and guides a person forward as it functions on an ongoing basis. The story demonstrates the activities of a part of the mind of which we are often unaware, a part that we must sometimes decode in order to improve mental health and engage therein with a higher consciousness within. We will ultimately have to landscape or architect this part in order to enjoy optimal mental health. More on that later.

In our day-to-day lives, this faculty is normally overlooked. We tend to focus on the verbal and conscious self. We know, though, we also have a part that allows us to possess knowledge in a wordless but visceral way. Brooks (2019) notes that we have words for this kind of knowing. We say, "she has a handle on it" or "he has definitely got the feel." We say that someone has "good taste." Implicit in this language is the idea that some knowledge is embodied. Sometimes you know something because you feel it in your bones.

Ever work on a problem, go to sleep and wake up with the answer you were reaching for? Other times, you have a clear intuition that becomes conscious. You are most grateful to have a faculty that seems to have a global comprehension of reality. Jordan Peterson speaks at length about this faculty. He calls it the implicit non-declarative memory, a faculty that others may call the Adaptive Unconscious or even the subconscious or unconscious mind. This faculty is vitally responsible for healthy adjustment and otherwise helps us master our world. Peterson spends a great deal of time explaining and describing the faculty. Our starting point is a deeper look at this faculty.

Your Other Half

Only when he no longer knows what he is doing does the painter do good things.
Edgar Degas

Well before you understood language, you needed a way of comprehending reality so as to navigate effectively. Last night you speared a piece of meat on a fork, tossed it into your mouth and chewed. There was a time, though, when that task was hard. Your best efforts left food all over your face and in your hair.

The implicit non-declarative memory is the part that stores procedural know-how. Over the course of years and with practice, this faculty got you balancing on your feet, walking, eating properly, effortlessly managing bathroom tasks. That faculty figured out how to ride a bike and drive a car. You deploy that faculty whenever you need to master some sort of procedural skill. It helps you read the patterns of reality. It acclimated to the force of gravity and you have been walking competently ever since. It registered social norms and integrated information about predictable aspects of the environment. It knows that fire is always hot. It memorized learnings, created expectancies and routinized motor behaviors so that you eventually became fluent doing many actions. To this day, it helps you ski, type, dance. It creates a 'macro' for what you need to do, so that you automate your actions, facilitating speed, achieving fluency.

And beyond it's motoric intelligence in navigating the tangible world, it also potentially grasps abstractions. Wolfgang Kohler quoted a physicist who said that many of science's important discoveries are made while in bed, in the bath or on the bus. Archimedes came up with the principle named for him when he stepped into the bathtub and noted the change in the water level, when stepping in. Einstein's Theory of Relativity was inspired by a dream that had him hurtling down a mountain at the speed of light. John Harvey Kellogg came up with his idea to produce a breakfast cereal that would aid digestion in the middle of the night. The subconscious faculty we are discussing can grasp reality in a way that supersedes the understanding of the rational mind; it subsequently informs the understanding of the rational mind. We saw an example of this in the case study mentioned above.

A Mind Out of Balance

If this faculty is underdeveloped, and the rational mind is over-developed, the result is rigidity. I recall a client of mine who had been diagnosed with Obsessive Compulsive Disorder. Initially he was taking showers throughout each day. A psychiatrist then taught him cognitive-behavioural strategies so he could argue with his compulsion. He mastered the technique. He could now defy the compulsions! He stopped all that showering. The problem did not end there, though. He started counting calories. Soon he was dangerously anorexic, on the verge of hospitalization. To help this young man therapeutically, we had to re-vivify the unconscious faculty.

In the grips of his pathology, this client was not unlike G.K. Chesterton's madman: "the madman is not the man who has lost his reason, the madman is the man who has lost everything but his reason . . . and his mind moves in a perfect but narrow circle." He ate with precision, intent to avoid weight gain and exercising to work off the calories from all the rice cakes. Over the course of three months, though, he brought in dreams which we analyzed and worked with, thereby communing with the unconscious. That part came to life.

Richard Rohr notes that:

> "the opposite of rational is not always irrational, it can be *transrational* or bigger than the rational mind can process; . . . The transrational has the capacity to keep us inside an open system and a larger horizon so that the soul, the heart, the mind do not close down inside of small and constricted space" (Rohr, 2010, Introduction).

For this client, the transrational perspective flourished; his resolve changed. Within a few months he decided to gain weight. He gained 25 pounds, channeling his detail-conscientious towards a new found interest in nutrition. He recovered nicely. For optimal mental health, this faculty needs to be developed.

Home of Neurosis, Bearer of the Map of Meaning

Despite all this faculty can do, despite the way it helps in a multitude of contexts, there is a problem: this part masters physical routines and sometimes bubbles up monumental insights, but at other moments it may be less than accurate. Sure, it has you covered with regards to driving your car. But some of the generalizations it makes relate to other aspects of existence: managing relationships, attitudes to authority, living within structures, or not. . . the list goes on and on.

This faculty actually builds a life map that it retains forever more and uses that map to guide your decisions and behaviours. That map is shaped by your life experiences, influenced by the particular personalities who made the largest impact on you growing up and by cultural norms or injunctions that left an imprint. This faculty silently and secretly came up with expectancies, "if *x*, then *y*" relating to what you could expect from a world that is ambiguous at times; also what you could expect from yourself, others, authority figures and life, more generally. It squirreled away beliefs and expectations that would serve as a map you would use as you moved forward in life.

Why was this necessary? Let's review from last chapter: Because at any given moment there is what you are familiar with and what is beyond your purview, what remains unknown to you. Initially, as infants, the world is mostly unknown. Gradually little corners of our world become more familiar, graduating to the status of 'known'. And then we move further afield, a little more, now. We leave the family home. We go to school. At every step we widen our exposure to the unknown and graduate to greater levels of competence with aspects of the world that were formerly unfamiliar. Living in a world that always has elements that are strange and unfamiliar, the subconscious collects learnings. It assembles a map, organizing what it knows, contributing to a feeling of stability, all of which makes it easier to continue the never-ending task of approaching the "vast nocturnal and star-studded ocean of all that we still don't know" (Rovelli, 2017, p. 17).

You Have a Map

So your subconscious mind has been maintaining a map for decades, out of your conscious awareness. There's a good chance that at least some parts of that map – much of which was sketched in before the age of 8 – are out of date and do not accurately represent the life space that is your world now. But you may still be using that same map to aim yourself forward. If things are not working out in your life, that map, harbored deep in the unconscious, may be at fault. Chances are, if you have a recurrent personal challenge that plagues you, you're stuck because this faculty, out of conscious awareness, retains learnings and beliefs that are unproductive, learnings you may not even realize lurk within.

Meet the bugaboo of mental health! This faculty sometimes bubbles up pure genius, best practices, whips up a meal like a pro, pulls off that dance move like nobody's business. At other times, this base of inspiration is . . . the address of neurosis! The faculty manufactures outdated visions of reality that sabotage progress. And despite evidence of certain corruptions, we continue to use the outdated map, driving the life project forward in ways that are maybe not always good. The faculty has served you so well for so many years ("it got me walking, driving, functionally employed, and effective in a myriad of ways. . . why should I doubt what it tells me is true?"), so you continue to follow its direction, even in the wake of feedback that is occasionally negative.

The Ideal of G-d

The focus of this book is Peterson's contention: that in this day and age the map cobbled together by this part of the mind is often deficient specifically as a consequence of living in a secular society. This faculty of the mind, he asserts, best learns via narrative, fable or through mythology, ideally that which is transmitted in the context of a sacred tradition or religion. Most religions use these modalities to communicate important values, deliberately using mediums that speak directly to this nonverbal faculty. Implicit teachings embedded in narratives and myths reinforce reverent values and provide a "unifying ethos," according to Peterson. These help to socialize children, establish a sanctioned direction so people understand how to move forward and promote harmony and order in society. In this day and age, the many narratives/movies/TV shows/novels are not communicating a singular, synchronized and evolved set of values. Their influence, then, can be disorganizing.

Peterson hypothesizes that these days, the task of "encountering chaos and turning it into habitable order," is particularly challenging because we must do so without the benefit of an inner structure that would normally be configured as a consequence of living in a reverent society. Peterson speculates that sacred traditions provide an a priori structure for consciousness, which means a person encountering chaos in the world at large would ordinarily (best) do so with an interior that is organized around guiding truths, an inner order that serves as a ballast. Pre-loaded with an organized worldview, a system of values, a healthy ideology and working ideals, all of these ensure a reasoned approach when navigating the chaos of this world.

With the benefit of an a priori structure, we are equipped to handle chaos. We can, like G-d in Genesis, order it or extract order from it. Without the benefit of that structure, we might succumb to chaos. After all, chaos has its own appeal. Many fall into rebellion, addictions, emotional or lifestyle dysregulation, taking up with the wrong crowd or dabbling with the usual lures that pull people away from the ordered, predictable ('boring', as per the secular worldview) life we otherwise maintain to access good health and mental health.

To tame the dragon of chaos, you need a structure to organize your efforts, a structure that anchors you to the the priority of order. For lack of such, Peterson asserts, individuals succumb to ideologies or substitute religions which may provide a structure, but not a healthy one (all of which was discussed at length in the last chapter). Unmoored from the grounding that weighty and significant moral systems would normally provide, many today are simply not well-rooted. In this environment, deprived of an optimal organizing structure, conglomerates or other interest groups can step in and push a narrative or ideology, one carefully selected to promote commercial interests (not yours). Given that others stand to profit from our own lack of structural integrity, we need to look more carefully at the structure which Peterson suggests best serves our cause.

Awakening the Ideal

According to Peterson, the structure that facilitates our task of bringing chaos to order is the ideal of G-d. Genesis 1:27 reads "So G-d created Man in His image, in the image of G-d He created him . . . " That line intimates that the structure of G-d and the structure of Man resemble each other. If the Divine infrastructure is intrinsically relevant to us, then societal disinterest and ultimate abandonment of the G-d ideal not only banishes G-d but, in some sense, ourselves. We may not know who, or how, to be. And that is one of Peterson's central points.

Beyond the secularism that governs the contemporary worldview, we can gauge the current status of the ideal of G-d, our Father in Heaven, by tracing what has happened to the Father archetype more generally over the last decades. This archetype has waned. Consider how father has been represented on TV over the decades.

If you are old enough, you remember “My Three Sons,” “Father Knows Best,” “Nanny and the Professor,” and “Leave it to Beaver.” In the 50’s, TV shows depicted father as a responsible, knowledgeable authority. Father was the patriarch at the helm of the family. As times changed, single females became the protagonists (“The Partridge Family,” “Mary Tyler Moore,” “Rhoda,” “Laverne & Shirley,” “Sex in the City”). Fathers/males were represented as non-essential, goofy, transient or unavailable (“I Love Lucy,” “Get Smart,” “Gilligan’s Island,” “Bill Cosby Show,” “Mork & Mindy,” “Mash,” “Simpson’s,” “Sony & Cher”). The authoritative father archetype lost its cache. The new male lacked gravitas. (“Three’s Company”, “Seinfeld”, “Friends”).

While the respect accrued to the Father archetype plummeted, simultaneously there was a spike in the number of single mothers raising families alone. There were less fathers in the picture. Dennis Prager (2019) cites Barack Obama who in 2008 said, “Children who grow up without a father are five times more likely to live in poverty and commit crime; nine times more likely to drop out of schools, and twenty times more likely to end up in prison.” Prager concludes that there are consequences when the archetype of Father fades out, since that archetype helps instill and enforce rules in a society. Without father, there is less order, more chaos. Or more shootings, as he conjectures, which was discussed in the Introduction. Prager hypothesizes that men in particular need the archetype of G-d. That archetype encourages healthy ways of channeling testosterone, the male hormone that gets men into trouble as per the research cited by Peterson. Toss the ideal and civility goes with it.

Others certainly see it that way. In Alcoholics Anonymous, the premise of the 12 steps is that the addict is powerless over the addiction and must admit that ‘a Power greater than self could restore me to sanity.’ The addict is to ‘turn his will and life over to the care of G-d’. *The Big Book*, AA’s central text, states, “It has been repeatedly proven among us that upon this simple cornerstone [the belief that there is a Power greater than myself

] a wonderfully effective spiritual structure can be built." There it is: the idea that the ideal of G-d provides a structure and that structure can lay the foundation for a healthy lifestyle. I hear Peterson saying, "That's exactly right."

The Structure

What is that structure provided by the G-d ideal? Let's review. The G-d ideal establishes standards, makes them very explicit and invites you into a covenant. It links you to that which is transcendent and requires you to cultivate discipline in order to achieve that which is noble. The G-d ideal serves as a judge, internalized within, which issues edicts when you fail to meet its standards. It stewards you forward, encouraging your efforts to bring order to chaos. For men and women both, it encourages the dynamism/ masculinity within. It awakens and animates the Father mentality, long after you've moved out of the parents' basement.

The G-d Ideal, then, heralds progress. It pulls you towards your potential. It does this by creating a consciousness of past, present and future, overriding what otherwise might be an exclusive focus on the present. The most important Hebrew name for the Divine, a four letter word that conjugates the verb 'to be', expresses the idea that He was, is and always will be. Even that name, then, communicates a structure to adherents, a structure that includes an awareness of time that goes beyond a simple consciousness of the present. The higher consciousness encoded in that name is the mandate to learn from the past, to sacrifice aspects of the present, all so as to maximize positive outcomes in the future. You can live in all three dimensions of time, at the same time! You can shoot yourself like an arrow and traverse the trajectory of past, present and future. Talk about transcendence!

> Human history is the long terrible story of man trying to find something other than G-d which will make him happy.
>
> CS Lewis

***Yin, Yang* & You**

Genesis 1:27 implies that G-d has dual facets: "G-d created Man in His image, in the image of G-d He created him, male and female He created them." The G-d ideal, then, embodies both masculine and feminine. As mentioned above, the ideal provides us with direction and giddy up, waking up and shaping the male aspect of the personality, what Jung called the Animus. But the ideal also possesses a feminine dimension and thereby models how we should activate our feminine nature (men and women, both). It also models the healthy integration of *both* facets of self. When we achieve that integration, we come to possess something we call '*good integrity*'. Therefore, part of the structure that the G-d ideal provides is direction how to manage and calibrate the two aspects of self, masculine and feminine.

Where do we see the integration of masculine and feminine in religious symbolism? Everywhere! The cross is comprised of the vertical line, connoting Divinity (masculine dimension), and the horizontal line connoting the material realm (feminine dimension). The Star of David shows two triangles merged, one pointing upward (the feminine) and one pointing downward (the masculine). The *Tai Ji* symbol famously represents *Yin* and *Yang*, the feminine and masculine, in a circular figure that has black and white, feminine and masculine, in an eternal synchronized orbit.

Indeed the premise of Chinese Medicine is that balance between these two dimensions of self is necessary for good health. Cold conditions, a deficiency/weakness of *Yin* or feminine, must be remedied with Heat (*Yang*). The individual feels cold. It will be important to 'heat up' the body and the sluggish metabolism. Deficiency of *Yang* results in weakness and apathy. Building the

Yin stimulates energy production (*Yang*) which awakens motivation.

With regard to Peterson's conception of reality, note that he acknowledges the core duality of creation. For example, Peterson discusses two major forces at play: culture, associated with the Father archetype, and chaos/nature, associated with the Mother archetype, as root forces with which we contend. Culture imposes order but, in excess, becomes tyrannical and controlling. Nature left undomesticated by 'culture', exposes us to freezing weather conditions and other hardships, unleashing a torrent of chaos on we who cannot withstand her ordeals without the aid of culture. Culture helps us manage Nature, and Nature prevents Culture from bloating into a force of oppression. So Peterson's formulation acknowledges the core duality at the root of creation, another expression of the Divine footprint.

Secondly, Peterson discusses the feminine and masculine archetypes which nest within the psyche. Peterson speaks to both of them. Regarding the masculine aspect, he urges activation: clean your room! Take responsibility! With regards to the feminine, he empowers its' particular sensibility, as well. Let's think of *Yang*/masculinity as a buoyant 'YES!' and *Yin*/femininity as a quiet and resolute 'no.' He counsels on the importance of delaying gratification, using best judgement to make decision and warms us to the concept of sacrifice. These are the priorities associated with *Yin*. The inner masculine bounds towards progress whereas the healthy feminine discriminates, introducing quality control. This latter facet warns what could go wrong, counsels what not to do and, when honed, animates the inner grit which powers self-discipline. The feminine helps you marshal your resources carefully. It is your 'better half,' you could say.

Responsibility and Sacrifice are the *Yang* and *Yin* in Peterson's playbook. He helps us podge together a G-d ideal by having us activate the right muscles and coaching us to use them in the right way. He tells us to have gratitude for both our privileges (sponsored by *Yang*, 'YES!') and our limitations (sponsored by *Yin*, 'no'). We must embrace/mobilize both aspects of our duality.

Peterson channels the archetype of father and assumes that role, especially speaking to a generation of young men who embrace the structure he promotes. That structure is premised on a worldview and values that deviate from the contemporary mentality advanced by corporate sponsors. The contemporary mentality emphasizes consumption; getting versus giving; Rights versus responsibility. The emphasis on rights has a person too *Yin*, too feminine, too 'what have you done for me lately?' Peterson insists that focusing on *Yang*, 'what can I do to make the world better?' will lead to a more meaningful life.

The Burning Bush

Remember the burning bush mentioned in the Hebrew Bible? You may recall that Moses noticed the bush and comprehends the miracle – the bush is not consumed. Say the story really happened (as many believers do). Initially, the scene probably looked unremarkable. Dry bushes burning in the Mid-Eastern sun must be par for the course. It would probably take some time for a person to notice the fire and realize the bush is not being consumed (Kushner, 2016).

Now think of the news. When it comes to fires in the wilderness, the outcome described in the bible is uncommon. Think California. Or British Columbia. We live in a world where *Yang* consumes *Yin*, fire devastates the corporeal. The city of Paradise, California burned to the ground. The nature of *Yang* is to combust. When it goes, it goes all the way. It takes down everything and everyone.

The Messianic vision, in contrast, is one that defies the law of nature – the lion will lie with the lamb. *Yang* and *Yin* will harmonically function as a unified, integrated system. *Yang* will accept the influence of *Yin*: the lion will *lie* with the lamb. *Yang* accepts the limitation represented by stillness characteristic of *Yin*/'no' so they both coexist nicely.

What does that look like in day-to-day life? The answer: Moderation. About his writing, Arthur Miller said, "I don't believe in draining the reservoir, do you see? I believe in getting up from the typewriter, away from it, while I still have things to say." The lion lies nicely with the lamb when that lion part of us dials down the burning drive to achieve to allow for rest and relaxation, when those are needed. Carl Jung said, "I realized that somebody who's tired and needs a rest and goes on working all the same is a fool."

If you think of it, the burning bush is the vision of rectification. We need the spark of Divinity, the fire, which animates the physical and sparks excitement and motivation. Masculinity can have – must have – full, dynamic expression – the fire must have a charge. *Yang* can live true to its nature and, *simultaneously*, not consume *Yin*. The Father archetype is the purveyor of this message: *Yang* can animate – within circumscribed limits – so that both *Yin* and *Yang* prosper. The alternative, of course, is called "burnout." Too much heat/*Yang!* The *Yin* withers, bullied and overwhelmed by the other faculty which overpowers.

One way Peterson represents this proper balance is his idea that one must not neuter or repress aggression. The goal is to be mindful of its corrosive power which burns bright . . .but keep it in your pocket. Only pull out your capacity to be vicious if you need to. That's another way the lion can lie with the lamb.

The vision of *Yin* and *Yang* functioning harmoniously is the healthy modus operandi for many spiritual systems. According to Ayurvedic medicine, the body possesses 7 chakras or energy centers. The upper 3, associated with the head, are construed as male. The lower three, associated with the lower part of the torso, are construed as female. The 4rth chakra, the heart, is the chamber where the two meet . . . and marry. The heart is the address of liberation and evolution. With progress, the lotus flowers in that chakra, resulting in a higher consciousness that only happens when the upper and lower chakras achieve a harmonious unity.

In the Jewish tradition, the healthy coexistence of the two facets of self is to be achieved by following Jewish law, called, in Hebrew, *halacha*. That word derives from the Hebrew word *holech*, the verb, to walk! Walking is the alternating animation of the right and left side of the body in the interest of moving productively forward! There it is again, the coordination of the right and the left, the *Yang* and the *Yin*!

In Judaism, the most central daily prayer embeds the same teaching. Called the *Sh'ma,* the 6 word evocation is translated in English as: "Hear, Oh Israel. the L-rd is Your G-d, the L-rd is One." In fact, the prayer includes two different and very specific names of G-d, which get lost in the translation. One name is that of the feminine aspect of Divinity, the other that of the masculine aspect. The prayer, then, heralds the unity of the Creator who possesses masculine and feminine aspects that inter-include to function as One, an intrinsic unity. That synthesis is something we work to accomplish, so that we truly make ourselves into the image of the Divine – that is our birthright. To work towards a state of harmony between the genders, we must architect a working partnership between *Yin* and *Yang* within each individual. When this is achieved, a person rectifies the world! And cultivates a unified, stable identity, in so doing!

Paradise Found: The State of Inter-inclusion

I'd like to suggest that as one works towards the goal wherein the two disparate aspects of selfhood are harmonized, a distinct deepening occurs. The personality changes. Perhaps this is the state referred to by Emerson when he wrote, "Standing on the bare ground – my head bathed by the blithe air and uplifted into infinite space – all mean egotism vanishes. I become a transparent eyeball; I am nothing. I see all; the currents of the Universal Being circulate through me. I am part or parcel of G-d."

The state is surely one of transcendence, which makes sense, if we use David Brooks conception of "transcendence as the feeling we get when living in accordance with some ideal" (2018, p. 104). No wonder Peterson speaks at such length when discussing the G-d ideal in his 'Psychological Significance of the Bible' lecture series. No wonder 4.4 million people have listened to that lecture, to date!

The Detractors

Insofar as the G-d ideal proscribes a choreography that unifies *Yin* and *Yang*, don't be surprised when competing ideologies specifically take down notions of differences between masculine and feminine.

Recently, a Google insider leaked Google's agenda to influence the outcome of the 2020 presidential election by shaping the thinking of those who use Google to search. He demonstrated Google's agenda to influence 'group think' in an interesting way.

Google populates suggestions when people type in the search bar. The informant typed in "men can" to show what popped up. Google provided the following suggestions: "have babies," "get pregnant," "have periods," "cook." Really?! This is what people are searching for? Whether men can have babies? The Google insider suggests these associations are programmed in to express a social justice narrative that decries gender roles or differences.

He also typed in, "women can". Google populated, "Do it," "do anything," "be drafted," "fly." The social justice narrative advocates a world where men get pregnant and women fly! This narrative defies any sort of normative definition for either *Yin* or *Yang*. That's called chaos.

"Masculine and Feminine, He Created Them"

In contrast to Google's vision, the structure Peterson recommends is one that has us working with our dual nature. To do so, we need to find a healthy working definition for each of our constituent parts, as a starting point. Confusing the intrinsic nature of *Yin* and *Yang* will obscure the destination. If we fail to construct solid structures, we will be more susceptible to ideologies which effectively advance somebody's else's vested interests.

"He who has a why to live can bear almost any how," said Nietzsche. Everything will ride on having the right structure, the healthy map of meaning. That's the why . . . and also the how. And if this structure relates to the ideal of G-d, finding the contours of this structure may be elusive. Where do we look?

I've written this book because virtually every sacred tradition provides adherents with a map of meaning that provides counsel and direction for those managing the duality we find in the world and in ourselves. Peterson has created a massive interest in young people who are casting their sights to the worlds of spirituality and religion, now that they understand there are maps to explore which might have what to offer them. Can there be a renaissance in religiosity? Can contemporary religions meet the needs of this target group, speaking their language and offering adult education that helps them find a home in the world of faith? Contemporary religionists will do well to learn what millennials are learning. It will help them speak to a young population who are awakening to the importance of faith and wondering about that next important step.

Notes

1. Much of this chapter appeared in *An Illustrated Guide for Using Jordan Peterson's 'Maps of Meaning' to Sort Yourself Out*, by Annette Poizner, MSW, Ed.D., RSW. In that book, I introduce a map of meaning of Divinity that derives from Kabbalah. That tradition provides roadside assistance for the person seeking a structural map of Divinity. As a secondary benefit, unpacking this map articulates the component parts of the psyche, all of which need to be developed to enjoy good mental health. The Kabbalah's map promotes self-insight and also coincides with

Peterson's teachings. Perhaps not surprisingly, the structure is introduced in Genesis, in the Garden of Eden, in the archetype of a tree that takes us to the definition of Life, itself.

3.

Changing Maps, Changing Minds

In this chapter, we will consider the specific protocol that each undergoes to build the initial map of meaning and also the anchors that keep the initial map rigidly in place long after it has outlived its utility. The context here: an army of Peterson fans have, with his encouragement, been dismantling their maps. People are taking his ideas to heart. They are cleaning their rooms! They are changing their maps!

These are people who have challenged their former narratives and are potentially re-thinking their former secular frame, shopping now for more wholesome influences. If religious institutions wish to appeal to those who are shaping a new worldview, it will help if they understand the mapping process in more detail. That will be the focus of this chapter.

Starting at a very young age, a child begins to assemble a working map of reality. One of the fathers of modern-day psychology, Alfred Adler, discussed the way people cultivate this map over time. He came up with a term for the map, calling it 'life style'.

For Adlerians, the life style of the individual refers to that individual's unique, consistent pattern of thinking, feeling, and acting. The life style is the person's 'organizing principle' or "rule of rules," as if each individual harbours a 'blueprint' which dictates consistent ways of coping or behaving (Shulman & Mosak, 1988, p. 3). In other words, the life style is the map each person uses to interpret reality and determine ways of acting or responding.

How is this life style assembled over time? The learning of a child occurs in a process of trial and error. The small child assesses reality, moment by moment, and gradually abstracts rules to live by. At first, say Shulman & Mosak, any given rule is treated like a hunch. With time, if the rule seems to work, it is elevated to the status of law. Those laws harden into full-fledged beliefs with staying power. At that point, the child, so convinced of the veracity of the law, will be drawn to perceive the world through the lens of his or her belief. He will find more and more validation of the law; certainty sets in. So the point here: the law is reinforced because a person perceives only that which supports his or her prevailing beliefs. As Einstein said, "Believing is seeing."

Say your map tells you that people are not to be trusted. You will be riveted each and every time people disappoint you and will fail to register times people are reliable and warrant trust. If your map tells you everybody in your midst cannot be trusted, you, too, will become untrustworthy ("why should I be reliable when they are not?"). The map dictates what you see, what you do, and ultimately shapes your life! This is why Peterson says it is so important to examine that map. Initially the map helps us to orient ourselves and generate generalizations about life so we can make predictions about what will happen next; later it limits our perceptions and functionally takes over, all this out of conscious awareness. Sadly, sometimes the map is effectively prescribing a life that involves enduring abuse, maintaining passivity, enduring isolation, etc. And so these circumstances occur in the present but relate to experiences the individual endured – and mapped out – at a much younger age.

"Our strongest beliefs were once new and even doubtable conclusions."

Ron Kurtz

Ideally, we should think of the early map as the "first edition," and take every opportunity to revise and update it, applying the learnings culled by life experience and other sources. Or we will hopefully have 'corrective experiences' that help us revise the map. Imagine the distrusting individual who has a relationship that is healing. The map will probably change. But what if the corrective experience doesn't happen? At the end of the day, as Ron Kurtz noted, children make the maps that they will use and rely on as adults. So often, changing the map is a DIY project which has to be undertaken later in life or it won't happen at all. When the effort is expended to read and then change the map, change ensues, bringing new outcomes and opportunities. Now – finally – the world can open up in new ways.

With all this it should be very clear: not having a healthy guiding ideology to inform parents and children as they move through the various stages of family life can have ramifications! Children are busy making their maps, whether we provide them with an organized, tried and true worldview or whether we cast them toward a hodge podge of influences: Cheetos commercials, video games, advertising, sitcoms. The kids sit at the foot of the TV, absorbed, activating a type of rapt attention that adherents would reserve for an audience with the Dalai Lama. The kids are absorbing messages, values which vary from one hour to the next. From all this, they are expected to come up with a reasonably effective map. Really? How?? And the map they come up with, they will cleave to, holding on for dear life. Oh, oh. This can't be good. Now we have a whole generation of people who were raised that way. And we are surprised that some people's maps are poorly constructed?

The first step: Peterson argues you need to access your map and so become aware of the values, beliefs and tendencies that drive you. Figure out where the map is pointing you. The ideal that you talk about may be worlds away from the life you are actually living. You may be courting mental health problems as a result.

If your map is off, if your premises, at least some of them, are falsehoods, you might fail where you otherwise would succeed.

And if a whole society of people have maps peppered with flawed perceptions and faulty evaluations, society itself can fall into social disarray, tyranny, violence, etc. Sadly, the world has many examples of just how bad things can get. Everybody needs to do their reckoning, to take a good look at the map that they have cultivated and to consider where their map is accurate, and where it is off and potentially leads them astray. Peterson says, "You aim yourself somewhere." Might as well figure out where that is.

Meet Your Map!

Peterson recommends that people do the personal work so that they 'find the North on their compass'. Each person needs to discover his or her unique path. But to do this a person has to access the map that lurks below, out of conscious awareness. Peterson recommends different techniques which can help a person discover their map and figure out which parts of the map work and which parts would best be updated. For example, he recommends his journaling program which has people doing a very substantial life review or consideration of their long-term goals. In the course of writing this lengthy journal, people gain much clarity about the map that guides them.

When Peterson discusses the map of meaning, people of faith may recall another prominent author who, decades ago, addressed the same topic in a ground-breaking book that addressed spirituality and psychology.

"The Road Less Traveled"

Back in the 1970's, *The Road Less Traveled: The New Psychology of Love, Traditional Values and Spiritual Growth,* achieved bestseller status, spending 13 years on the New York Times bestseller list. In some ways it was the 70's version of Peterson's *12 Rules*. In it, he articulated ideas that sound like classic Peterson. He wrote about the need for each person to live a life dedicated to the truth. He stated that the person who had a clear perception of reality would be more successful in life, whereas those who failed to understand the contours of reality would make poor decisions and get derailed. For Peck, this perception of reality was a map of life that each person cultivated and used to negotiate reality.

Peck pointed out that people must constantly revise the map they have made so it will remain accurate over time, despite changing circumstances and realities – both internal and external. Peck asserted that many neglect to do so because revising the map is often painful. Refusing to amend and update their map, many will ignore or reject new information, even "crusade" against it, preferring to maintain a narrow and outdated worldview. For Peck, this reluctance to change the map results in many of the ills in society. (Peck, 1978)

Change Ain't Easy

Peterson, too, describes the phenomenon whereupon people are reluctant to be corrected if some aspect of their worldview would seem to be flawed. He notes that arguing with someone about a belief they hold dear can prompt a strong angry response, even rage which would seem irrational. After all, why not just admit their mistake and move on?

To quote Peterson on this issue: "when you poke people in the axioms they get upset… Almost like they've been clinging to a raft and you have just pulled out the logs from below and now they will drown . . . why should people be so afraid to move beyond their ideological systems?"

He answers: "we want our protective stories to stay intact. We want to know that our global conceptualizations about reality are accurate and we organize ourselves and our thought structures on that basis. Removing a brick can bring down the whole house." Peck and Peterson agree. It's a painful experience when our conceptualizations are challenged. There are scary implications:

What if I can't trust myself as a knower? What if my map is completely wrong?

Peterson reflects, "You have to be laid low before the new revelation can make itself manifest. . . .you have to figure out what's wrong [about your thinking] in order to figure out what guiding wisdom you need to access."

"Enlightenment consists not merely in the seeing of luminous shapes and visions, but in making the darkness visible. The latter procedure is more difficult, and therefore, unpopular."

Carl Jung

Why is there pain associated with making vital changes in the map of meaning? Doing so will change the trajectory of life – in a good way – and yet the pain of admitting a mistaken belief will deter some from allowing any modification in the old map.

The Talmud (Niddah 30b) teaches that in the womb, an angel spends the duration of the pregnancy teaching the child wisdom – providing a comprehensive and accurate map of meaning – while a candle burns over the head of the baby, allowing it to see from one end of the world to the other (with such an accurate map, the child possesses a full, complete understanding. In this case, the map is so accurate it is the territory). Then delivery begins. Right before the baby emerges, the angel gives the baby a smack right above the upper lip, creating the indent below the nose that is known as the philtrum. That blow causes the loss of all the knowledge. The individual is tasked to reclaim all that knowledge over the course of a lifetime and thereby to recreate that completely accurate read of reality. The text adds that when the individual dies, he or she promptly meets the same angel who asks, "Did you bring down the wisdom I taught you?" [1]

The Talmud's conception is interesting, because the premise here is that the child undergoes the loss of the comprehensive map in a painful, sudden and shocking manner. If that loss occurred in a state of duress, perhaps the process of fixing corruptions in an inaccurate map also, by necessity, occurs in a similar state, accounting for the pain associated with correcting flawed ideas and beliefs.

As Peterson and Peck understand, the pain associated with new learning is too much for some. Feeling that we have a rational understanding of the world creates a sense of security. And holding certain beliefs may bring another benefit: group identification. Peterson points out that group identification helps us manage the anxiety associated with the unknown aspect of reality. So there are different reasons a person may be reluctant to revise the map of meaning. Another relates to perceptual biases. Interesting research shows the degree to which we will ignore aspects of reality that are not duly noted on our map.

Sigh. Everything that we are learning makes the case for exposing children to a spiritual tradition and living within such a framework when they are young. If you meet those kids later and try and introduce a faith-based map, they will be less inclined to modify the prevailing map. They have been wielding it for years. I've heard parents defend the idea that they don't want to raise their kids with a faith, thereby allowing their kids to choose for themselves later. A big mistake, it seems to me . . .

"Believing is Seeing"

If you frequently listen to Peterson, you have heard him describe this study. Students are tasked to watch a short video in which players toss around a basketball. The subjects are told to count how many times the ball is tossed. But there is a catch. There are two teams in the video. The players wearing white are throwing the basketball to others wearing white. There's a team of players wearing black who are throwing another basketball to other players wearing black. The subjects are specifically asked to only count the number of times somebody on the white team throws their ball to somebody on the white team. This task requires more concentration because subjects have to disregard the ball being thrown by and to players wearing black. Subjects complete the task and submit the number of times the ball was tossed. Then they are asked, "did you see the person dressed in the Gorilla outfit?"

Indeed, at one point in the three minute video a tall person walked out wearing a Gorilla costume, thumped his chest a few times and then exited. Subjects were so busy tracking how many times the ball was tossed, they didn't notice the 'gorilla!' Back to Einstein: "Believing is seeing!" Confirmation bias refers to our tendency to only perceive that which we expect. And owing to this human tendency, once you have formed your map of reality, you may not notice anything which contradicts that map. In an often cited quote, 17th century philosopher-scientist Francis Bacon spoke of this human tendency. He wrote,

> The human understanding, once it has adopted opinions, either because they were already accepted and believed, or because it likes them, draws everything else to support and agree with them. And though it may meet a greater number and weight of contrary instances, it will, with great and harmful prejudice, ignore or condemn or exclude them by introducing some distinction, in order that the authority of those earlier assumptions may remain intact and unharmed.

Why are people so locked, closed to registering that which disproves their maps? Remember the world is constructed to mask or cloak the Divinity at its root. The denial mechanism is part of the apparatus put in place which allows the façade to continue. To the degree a person resolves his or her deficiencies is the degree to which a person will have clearer vision, recognize G-d (aka Truth) and have an easier time registering errors and amending the map (with less pain involved!). Raising a child within a spiritual framework will go a long way to helping facilitate this clarity. Doing so helps a child see beyond the mask of nature, to quote Tatz (1995). It helps them see beyond the material world, so they can understand that, in actuality, this is a world of action and a world of value.

Peterson points out that those who fail to notice that which disproves their map will usually bear negative consequences – falling into chaos – later. Imagine the person who justifies a vice like smoking. Perhaps his map tells him that he has made many responsible and productive life choices, therefore he is allowed . . no, *deserves* the physical pleasure he gets from smoking. If later this individual experiences a health crisis related to smoking, he may become ill, need treatments or even face death. Had he made a sacrifice when he initially learned of the risks associated with smoking and endured the hardship of breaking the addiction back then, he would have weathered a lesser sacrifice and perhaps avoided a worse sacrifice later.

Any psychotherapist can tell you people are attached to the map that they spent a lifetime using. Our maps influence not just what we say and do, but what we see! Peterson has encouraged those who follow his work to spend the time figuring out where their map points them. People who have taken his message to heart have realized that upgrading the map will bring good benefits. They show up in Jordan Peterson Facebook pages keen to share their ideas and discuss strategies for moving forward in new directions.

In the past, individuals undergoing this sort of life review – a dramatic process one client called a 'birthquake' – would consult a clergy leader. Today, we are more inclined to think that psychotherapy is a venue for working through changes in the individual's map of meaning. This certainly can be a task to address in therapy, but today many mental health providers are grounded in a strongly secular value system.

My perception is that psychotherapy has become a religion in itself, with the therapist as the minister. I urge people to be very mindful when selecting a therapist. The therapist you choose dictates your path. Is this person's worldview one you want to absorb? And if you seek psychotherapy, will this delay a quest for spiritual affiliation and exploration? That spiritual affiliation will provide an anchor in life and will help populate the map of meaning in good ways. A lifetime affiliation with a therapist might not provide the same degree of benefit. Not to say that it is never appropriate to see a therapist. But one ideally should grow roots in some sort of religious or spiritual community; psychotherapy is not a replacement for that.

How Peterson Recommends Surveying One's Own Map of Meaning

People who find themselves exploring spiritual communities may have done Peterson's journaling exercise, the Self Authoring Suite which has participants contemplating their life history, their goals and more. As mentioned earlier, Peterson reports that research shows that when first year university students in residence were run through the protocol and did the extensive journaling, the rate of dropouts in first year went down significantly and the marks of the students were higher than those in the control group.

They may have visited Peterson's website where people can fill out a questionnaire and get a report of findings on personality style based on the Five Factor Personality Test. Getting a comprehensive report and learning about the degree of introversion or extraversion, neuroses, conscientiousness, agreeableness and other traits has been a useful exercise which helps people better understand who they are and provides insight into the map of meaning.

Many have stretched themselves by reading and learning. Peterson provides a lengthy reading list and listening to his many talks and classes also has helped people make changes to their map of meaning, by virtue of the new information they learn.

And then they are ready for the next step. How can your organization or religion meet them where they are and speak their language? Can you offer courses which are 'Psychology 101' from the perspective of your religion or denomination? What about a course which, like Dennis Prager's book on happiness, claims to be a "Human Nature Repair Manual"? Can you design programs presenting the map of meaning put forward by your denomination or sect? Can you present Peterson's ideas, then show areas of agreement or disagreement, informed by the great thinkers of your spiritual tradition?

When you meet Peterson fans they will tell you that they studied his work and started making changes. A guy cleans his room, or maybe tweaks his self-care regime – cooking, sleep habits, etc. – with more conscientiousness. He starts treating himself with as much care as he would attend the needs of someone he valued. He's triggered a virtuous cycle wherein one positive change spurs the next positive change, and so on. Things got better. How could involvement in your community or practice take his or her progress to the next level?

Freshening Up that Map!

Peterson's message, again and again, is that "each person needs a path that justifies the tragedy of life." He would have us all dabble with the unknown, sway from the old path if it hasn't been working so well. He has been a great tour guide for many. Some are now standing at the curb waiting for the next teacher. Is that you? Can you pick up where he leaves off? Can you introduce Peterson followers to new theorists, new ideas, new formulations? Can you help them further upgrade the map of meaning that they are in the midst of renovating? Peterson introduces ancestral wisdom that can help people make new decisions about how they think about life. Perhaps you can be a partner in that project and help his followers on their path to access the supernal meaning that undergirds the creation and their lives.

Notes

1. Interestingly, the Greeks also harbour an idea that a soul has access

to all wisdom prior to incarnating.

4.

Peterson's Map of Meaning

As we begin to look specifically at many of Peterson's core teachings, I'd like to mention Peterson's overriding priority, the task of bringing order to chaos. The concept of chaos we can link to the second line of Genesis:

"when the earth was astonishingly empty, with darkness upon the surface of the deep, and the Divine Presence hovered upon the surface of the waters"

That line relates two primary aspects of creation:

> a) a lower dimension which is a 'mass' of empty darkness or as Peterson calls it, " a formless and potential chaos." That chaos will be, says Peterson, the matter "from which all things will emerge and rise." Water implies movement. We might expect water to be affected by the hovering movement that occurs above. Depth, emptiness and darkness would seem to imply the absence of order or intelligence.
>
> b) The second constituent of this creation is suspended above the first: the intelligence, the Divine Presence, hovering above. Early in the creation narrative, therefore, we find the vertical dimension referenced, bringing an association to the hierarchy, but more on that later.

The third aspect of creation is the intermingling of the above two. For example, with the creation of Adam, the Divinity penetrates the lifeless body, breathing into and bringing life/order to a lump of clay. Fusing Divinity with the physical has a functional byproduct: the human can stand, speak, name the animals and so mimic the verbal declarative acts of his Creator. Like Father, like son.

As we follow the text, we see that at the outset of any creation, crude physicality always needs tweaking. Each facet of creation is then landscaped, organized, ordered; then it works! Only then is it 'good' by Divine account. The act of fusing the spiritual and the physical will become the universal strategy we use to aim at 'good'. In line 2, though, the Divine is not fused with the creation. He hovers above. Physicality and Divinity are separate. The word good is not associated with this stage of the creation process.

How do things play out? The physical world, as per the last verse, has water covering the entire surface of the world. In order to move past that chaotic state, a process of ordering has to take place. G-d has to clean his room! He pushes the water to the side, making way for land but this only occurs after He separates the upper waters from the lower waters. More ordering!

When the sun and the moon are created, there is chaos. Note that in the text, the sun and the moon are initially described as two great lights. Then Genesis 1:16 continues, "the great light to rule by day and the small light to rule by night." What happened? The Talmud teaches there was a dispute. When you have two great lights there will be an inevitable power struggle. Chaos! G-d subsequently reduced the moon, creating a clear hierarchy that resolved the immediate conflict. [1]

The animals are created. They are ordered when Adam gives them their names. Speech has a lot to do with how we order the world. Or as Peterson points out, "conscious articulation helps bring something into actualization . . . we can't get a grip of something till it has a name."

You see the pattern every where you look. Wheat in its natural state is not terribly useful. You can't eat it. It takes a lot of processing/ ordering to derive value from it. Ever try to bite into a raw rutabaga? It takes serious cooking to make that thing edible. And it took quite a bit of ordering to invent electricity, light bulbs, computers, etc.

What about human development? Initially, as children, we are chaotic! No wonder our early maps of meaning are inadequate! Landscaping is required! We have to sort ourselves out, integrating the influence and intelligence of the Divine Presence, aka the influence of parents, authority figures, teachings, teachers, etc. That presence looms above, overhead, so each person has to look higher on the hierarchy to access somebody that has more clarity, someone who can direct and guide. If we find role models or teachers who will help us access the Divinity that hovers overhead, we can actualize our potential. Those figures, then, are emissaries of Divinity.

We will need principles to guide the ordering task, especially given the baseline chaos that exists. What teachings will help us tame and order the chaos so we can understand reality, master it and so integrate the Divinity that hovers overhead? I'd like to suggest those principles are the ones Peterson teaches, accounting for the popularity and relevance of his work.

Peterson brings out these core insights in an age characterized by terrible confusion aka chaos. ADHD addles the mind of the young, dementia invades the elderly, gender no longer plays a role in defining our lives. A lot of the markers we used to use to organize life are gone. Remember when all stores were closed on Sundays? Remember when night was a time for sleep because there wasn't much else you could do? Hillman and Ventura (1992) comment, "Twenty-four hour bank call-ins and automatic tellers are in themselves insignificant details of contemporary life. But as part of a pattern, it speaks of a people increasingly coaxed to live without pattern in terms of services, while they bemoan the loss of pattern in their morality, their love-life, their thought…(p. 116)." Contemporary life is disorienting.

The principles that Peterson has been teaching seem to be helping people. He suggests you can use them to cope with chaos and confusion. He claims using these principles can help you "turn chaos into habitable order." Some of these ideas could be called 'common sense'. But he is a breath of fresh air, to bring my Genesis metaphor forward! He gives us a language for all this and then we can stand, like Adam, and name our world! When we do that, we sort ourselves out!

Let's look specifically at some of Peterson's central teachings. If we have integrated faulty understandings about reality into our map/worldview, Peterson "pokes us in the axioms." He challenges our conceptions of reality, triggering insight that can help the project at hand!

I present this chapter so you can get a feel for what Peterson's followers have been learning and what they have been processing. This information can help you understand their frame of reference and lets you figure out how to present your teachings in a way that is as seamless as possible.

The Core Dimensions of Life

To flesh out Peterson's ideas, I'd like to present them in a format that is my own. Consider that by the time the Creation narrative is done, the life space has familiar dimensions: vertical, horizontal, field of depth, and if we consider a three dimensional cube as a metaphor for the life space, there is also another dimension: the center point, hidden in the middle of the cube. The center point is situated centrally and equidistant from each of the six sides of the cube. You could say that the cube finds its unity through the center point because it serves as the common point of connection for each side, connecting them all.

I'd like to suggest that so many of Peterson's insights are, at core, intrinsically relevant and true to reality, that we can organize these teachings and show their correspondence to the familiar dimensions of the physical world: depth, width and height. Note that I am putting his learnings in this format, which I think is handy, but that formulation is not one that he discusses in his books or lectures.

The Vertical Axis

According to Peterson, complex biological creatures have to move towards things in the world in order to stay alive. We move towards food, people, experiences that we perceive will make our lives better. The fact that life has us moving forward as we pursue our wants and needs will relate to depth of field, to be discussed soon. But because we reach to achieve goals that we project out into the future, we now have the necessity of hierarchies. Hierarchies relate to the vertical dimension of life.

We said earlier that there is a hierarchy of value. Some things are worth pursuing and other outcomes are best avoided. The positive aspect of living with hierarchies is that we have the possibility of aiming at and achieving desirable outcomes. If there is a higher goal, there is also a less attractive alternative. When people have something to aspire to, their lives have meaning. With no outcome to strive towards, life feels useless. So in many ways the hierarchy adds quality to our lives.

But hierarchies introduce their own set of problems. Inevitably, a small group of people will find their way to the top of the hierarchy, say, of competence, while the majority will be dispossessed, marginalized at the bottom, caught up in less favourable circumstances. Further, there is the potential that those at the top abuse their power, resulting in tyranny. So hierarchies come with imperfect outcomes. Peterson points out we have to monitor the more unfortunate and inevitable negatives which come into play when dealing with hierarchies.

In his book, *12 Rules for Life*, Peterson writes one chapter about the topic of hierarchies and calls his rule on the topic, "stand up straight with your shoulders back." Indeed, standing up straight has a person inhabiting the vertical axis. The person who stands up straight will exert self-discipline and governance in other aspects of life, too. He or she tries harder, putting in the extra effort to "climb the corporate ladder" or other ladders of competence. The vertical dimension is an inevitable part of the landscape and he who submits to that fact will set high goals, cultivate role models, and healthy relationships to authority figures. We expect more wins for these people. Next we can consider the horizontal axis.

The Horizontal Axis

If we think about the body, we can notice that forward movement, walking, requires alternating movements between the right and left side of the body; you have to put the right foot forward, followed by the left, and so on. The vertical axis would have us reach for the stars, way up there, but the horizontal axis, to keep us grounded, wants us to deploy both faculties, the right and the left, sequentially, to stay grounded.

When Peterson talks about the horizontal axis – right and left – he is talking about political orientation/temperament. It's no coincidence that right wing and left wing imply something spatial and more specifically relating to a body, as in the wings of a bird. In fact, these two orientations represent the extremes along a continuum that I am calling the horizontal axis. Along these lines, some mystical traditions locate different tendencies in the personality in different parts of the body; the left and right axis relate to a continuum which has expansive, creative generosity at one end of the spectrum and contractive, legalistic tendencies at the other end. In common parlance, we refer to these polarities as extroversion and introversion. One could argue that every personality needs to master both of these capacities or orientations, while also recognizing that each person will have more of one than the other.

According to Peterson, the right wing is a political orientation that values hierarchies and focuses conscientiously to implement them. The left-wing sensibility offers checks and balances, vigilant to inequities that can occur when hierarchies exist. This group is sensitive to the plight of those who are marginalized at the bottom of the hierarchy and alert to potential abuse of power at the top of the hierarchy. If the right wing is unfettered, tyranny can result. On the other hand, if the left-wing is unchecked the hierarchy is eroded under policies which favour the marginalized but the economic viability of the state may be tested.

Peterson describes the primary psychological traits that research associates with members of each group. The right wing is characterized by "conscientiousness," which includes sub-traits like orderliness, logical thinking and a tendency to be highly responsible. Skilled at limit-setting, this personality is risk averse, always mindful of what can happen when boundaries are not maintained. This type possesses excellent executive skills and so is drawn to roles such as manager or administrator.

"Openness" is the trait that corresponds to the left-wing mentality. This personality is creative, potentially rebellious and motivated to innovate new protocols and hierarchies, the classic entrepreneur type. Society needs both types to thrive, asserts Peterson, but they best function in dynamic dialogue versus pitted against each other in a highly polarized tug-of-war.

"If we can stay with the tension of opposites long enough – sustain it, be true to it – we can sometimes become vessels within which the divine opposites come together and give birth to a new reality."
Marie-Louise von Franz

With regards to the horizontal axis, we can appreciate there are two disparate faculties that each person possesses, and even if each person has a favored way of approaching the world, we need to deploy sometimes one, sometimes the other. We have to view both faculties as important and necessary for the human project to succeed. Walking is the metaphor that represents the harmonic function of both faculties working in synch to move things forward. In fact, The proper execution of the two disparate aspects of self, which has them both developed and executed in a way that is inspired, is the goal of alchemy. This is the topic of volume 2 of this series, called, *An Illustrated Guide for Using Jordan Peterson's Insights Regarding Divinity & the Map of Meaning to Sort Yourself Out.*

Depth of Field

The depth of the cube introduces the dynamic of living in the context of time. Note that we understand time spatially. The past seems to be behind us, the future before us. Think of life as requiring us to navigate the space between the center point (representing the present, where you are right now) and a point forward in the future, moving you 'out there'. Will we focus on instant gratification and therefore be stuck in an eternal, unchanging present? Or will we live with a future orientation? Peterson tells us "not to sacrifice who we could be for who we are right now." Better to spend time and energy today to accomplish some objective in the future. Or, as he advises us, "Take your future self into account."

This idea takes us back to our original premise: reality is not a world of things. Reality is a world of action. At any given moment we have our current state in the present and a more desired state which lives, at least in our imagination, in the future. Living properly in the depth of field/ the framework of time, requires us to take purposeful action; in so doing we create a meaningful life. Culture, mythology, popular fairytales and biblical stories introduce us to the archetype of the hero, the one who delays gratification and purposely takes decisive action in order to achieve a desirable goal.

"The smallest good act today is the capture of a strategic point from which, a few months later, you may be able to go on to victories you never dreamed of."
CS Lewis

Once we understand that action is necessary, we have to determine what kind of action to take. Note that the Asian classic, *Tao Te*

Ching, translated as the "Classic of the Way's Virtues," is an Eastern guide to practices and life choices that constitute the ideal 'way' of being or behaving. The Tao itself refers to a cosmic universal pattern which animates the superior 'way', hence it is referred to as 'the way'. In another ancient tradition, Jewish law is called "*Halacha*" in Hebrew, derived from the word "*holech,*" the Hebrew word for 'walk'. Jewish law, then, proscribes a way of walking, a way of progressing. Peterson notes that all religions prescribe their version of the ideal way to advance in life. This allows us to move through time with more direction, while maintaining ourselves purposefully on the straight and narrow.

Why straight? Straightness is a virtue in the sacred traditions compared to the gentle curves that characterize nature. Think about it. If you stand on a curved road, you look behind you and you can't see where you've come from. You look before you and you can't see where you're going. Straightness represents alignment (find the line in there?) of speech, deed and heart. Within the line we find the 'I', the organized experience of selfhood, finding "oneself," or 'one self', the healthy, unified identity, the prototype of psychological health. [2] We will revisit the idea of the straight line in the next chapter.

The Center Point

Rumi said, "Yesterday I was clever, so I wanted to change the world. Today I am wise, so I am changing myself." Peterson advances this idea and issues the battle cry to the young: "Clean your room!" He understands that young people see many problems in the world and, compelled by idealism and the energy of youth, can charge into the task of 'changing the world'. But there is a problem. World problems are much bigger than any given 20 year old! And further, "it is easier for things to go really wrong than it is for them to go right." Implementing so called global 'solutions' can have all sorts of unanticipated negative consequences.

Given all the barriers, Peterson has a better idea: change your own "local landscape." Fix what is right in front of you! Your room, your field of being, "which is an externalization of your mind," notes Peterson. Get rid of the rubbish! Straighten up what you can straighten up! Organizing your room organizes your psyche, says Peterson. It makes you more effective, overall, maybe even makes you better at work or slightly more useful to your family. So don't fix the world! "Fix what is in your domain of competence," he says. "Build a microcosm of perfection with what you have at hand."

Then he adds, maybe, once you have gone through all your stuff – and now you know how hard it is to do one simple project from start to finish – only at that point do you hesitantly "extend a tentacle out beyond [your little life space] and tap something in the real world [to try to change it] . . . gently!!" Good advice about how to live in the center point, the sweet spot of your reality.

Note that we are all ideally treading paradox. As per above, we are to live in the depth of field which means we are always to have a future focus. We should be looking around and seeing what is wrong in the world and what needs to be fixed. But at the same time, we need to be anchored in the center point. First, fix yourself! Don't get lost in the depth of field, shooting yourself out into the environs to fix everybody else. Start with self-repair! And conversely, once you sort yourself out, then you further extend into the 'depth of field'. Maybe there's something in the world out there that you really can change. Don't only live in the center point! And don't only throw yourself wildly forward traversing the depth of field but oblivious to what is near at hand that needs to be managed! The complexity of living!

Take Care of Yourself

Another Peterson principle that relates to the center point is the idea that you should treat yourself like you would treat somebody whom you value. When he comes up with this idea, he is tackling what we might call a masochism that quietly plays a part of the culture, a tendency to self-deny. And if we live in a secular culture, maybe that masochism makes sense. If you lack Divinity in your constitution, there may be no reason you should provide extra special care for yourself or your body.

Imagine: Your blood sugar is falling, or you really have to go to the bathroom, but the impulse is, "let me just finish this task." It truly is bedtime. You can't keep your eyes open. But you push forward, "let me just finish this." By the time you finish, the adrenaline has kicked in. Now you are wide-awake. What do you do? Maybe get more work done. Or take a sleeping pill. Neither is the good way to go.

Making the right choice from the position of the center point means factoring the body's experience and best interests into decisions you make at any moment of decision. Peterson knows that there is a tendency to self-neglect. He writes a chapter of the *12 Rules* book so as to help you notice the pattern, catch it, and make new decisions that enhance your life and your experience of well-being. When you make responsible decisions in the center point, the here and now, you keep yourself in good form so you are in shape to exert and work towards your goals, as they relate to the vertical axis mentioned earlier.

The Teachings

It seems to me that some of Peterson's most important teachings pertain to the above mentioned aspects of life (and this certainly is not an exhaustive list). In his work, Peterson analyses many fairytales, movies, creation myths, classic literary works, all to demonstrate the teachings that are embedded within each narrative. These teachings are accessed by the less conscious self when reading these works, but are brought to our conscious awareness when Peterson points out the various metaphors and hidden meanings embedded in each story. He suggests that if we populate our personal life maps with these ideas, our lives are better for it. Peterson's followers seem to be finding veracity in that claim.

There are signs that these growth-oriented individuals are motivated to find other rules and systems which they can successfully use to improve their lives. If religious institutions can show the wisdom of their traditions and the utility in working with these traditions, a generation of young people might engage further, bringing excitement and vigor to the religions that they had earlier ignored or rejected.

Notes

1. Note that even G-d Himself recognized that this move was problematic; that He was guilty of a misdeed for imposing this power differential. Somehow reducing the station of the moon was still warranted for the betterment of the world's function. The Talmud discusses this issue, which is not a matter of concern here but may be a topic for discussion in a later volume
2. These are ideas I heard articulated by Rabbi Dr. Akiva Tatz in his online lectures.

5.

Take a Walk with a Line

Artist Paul Klee, teaching drawing, used to instruct his students to "take a walk with a line." His comment always resonated with me. My entry into the mental health field was unusual. While abroad, I had learned of a clinician who analyzed handwriting and drawings. Fascinated, I went for an assessment. The experience – and feedback – was life-transforming. One year later, I made my way back to Israel for psychotherapy with that clinician. Over the course of that therapy I studied the psychology of handwriting, learning with a practitioner. So from my current perspective – as a practitioner of clinical graphology – I can tell you that as soon as people pick up a pen they are, effectively, taking a walk with a line.

Jordan Peterson would probably say that life itself involves nothing less than taking a walk with a line. When he asks you to consider where you are aiming, he is effectively pointing out that we are linear beings. Our trajectory is a straight line. If you aim yourself somewhere, five years down the line, that's probably where you're going to wind up. Unlike four-legged animals with their horizontal existence, we are vertical, like walking lines. It's no coincidence that the personal pronoun in the English language is represented as a straight line. That's our ideal: to be aligned in thought, word and deed. Peterson himself is a straight shooter. How sad that certain cultures within our society construe "straight" as pejorative. To be straight is to be ethical versus deceiving, to be transparent versus secretive. There's a connotation of symmetry, tradition, precision. These are admirable traits.

In my last book, An Illustrated Guide for Using Jordan Peterson's Insights Regarding Divinity to Sort Yourself Out, I explored the G-d ideal through the lens of Kabbalah and handwriting. If I might share a couple of noteworthy handwritings. In that book I pointed out that people will often embed the archetype with which they resonate within their script, an expression of identification, value and allegiance. By way of example, please note the impressive signature of Dr. Jordan Peterson.

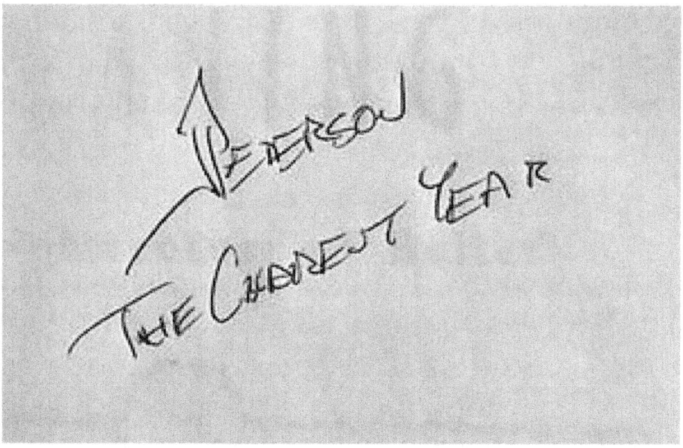

Signature of Dr. Jordan Peterson

In Peterson's signature, the arrow pointing upward, representing the imperative of climbing the hierarchy, is embedded right at the start of his signature. Notice in making letters he favours the line as the constituent part, preferring to make, for example, a capital E which allows him to use lines versus, say, using the cursive form which requires a rounded stroke. You don't have to be a graphologist to see that upward pointing arrow at the start of the signature, or to notice that the signature itself thrusts across the page or to register its legibility, all which demarcate the individual who gives it to you straight.

Signature of Prime Minister Justin Trudeau

By way of comparison, note the signature of Canada's Prime Minister Justin Trudeau. Where Peterson's signature is straightforward, Trudeau's is convoluted. Trudeau's archetype is the circle associated with community-mindedness, emotional warmth, inclusiveness. The circle is a nest whereas the line points towards progress.

Peterson is an ambassador of the line and, I would argue, the line is what we must master if we hope to cultivate discipline and if we hope to organize ourselves to achieve our goals, to get from here to there. We need to deploy the line if we wish to be successful.[1]

Judaism subtly alludes to the importance of the line as an archetype that provides the structure for our lives. As mentioned earlier, the most important name for Divinity is a four letter word which is an amalgamation of the three tenses: was, is and will be. Divinity, itself, then, relays the concept of the line, requiring us to be mindful of the past, making choices in the present while living with the future goal in mind. There you have it, the three points on the line: the beginning, middle and end. In Hebrew, the word for truth is a three letter word. The first letter is the first letter of the Hebrew alphabet. The second letter is the middle letter of the Hebrew alphabet. The last letter is the last letter of the Hebrew alphabet. Again we find the three points on that line. Truth is linear. Not curved. Not rounded. Very straightforward.[2]

So the point of this volume is effectively to say that it's not so easy to figure out how to animate the archetype of the line in our lives. We are complicated beings. We have different drives competing for satisfaction. And monotheistic religions, recognizing the unity at the root of creation, provide lessons, narratives, rituals, methods to help adherents master that archetype. It may be that family lineage is an important factor that might dictate which sacred path is appropriate for which individual. Or not. But one of the most important quests in life is going to be to adhere to a system that can help a person master the art of living the line. Each tradition has its own prescribed formula.

Peterson has carefully articulated the flaws associated with living in a secular society. I hope this book helps facilitate the growth of former secularists who are searching for a spiritual path. I pray these individuals find books, role models and clergy who will help them achieve the most optimal alignment with higher self, with Divinity, and with others. Each of us, really, is just trying to figure out one thing, and one thing, most centrally: which way up?

Notes

1. I have analyzed these and other handwritings in my second volume. What I might add here, as a tangent: In Trudeau's signature we find imagery of a cartoon character peering off to the right, wearing glasses, big nose, no mouth: a cartoon character, watching. All the rounded strokes and decorations signal 'the performer'. He watches us watch him. In contrast, Peterson is the penultimate doer, the straight shooter. This is the archetype we are to emulate. Not the performer/watcher who plays to the audience, but the one who expresses core truths with drive, precision, well-aimed.
2. Since the writing of this volume, I have written another specifically speaking to the structure of the line which, I suggest, is the core structure of self, as evidenced in the teachings and writings of Dr. Jordan Peterson. That book is entitled, *In Good Standing: Using Jordan Peterson's Insights on the Structure of Self to Sort Yourself Out.*

Bibliography

Alcoholic Anonymous (2001). *The Story of How Many Thousands of Men and Women Have Recovered* from Alcoholism (Fourth Edition). New York City: Alcoholics Anonymous World Services, Inc.

Brooks, David (2019). *The Second Mountain: The Quest for a Moral Life*. New York City: Random House Publishers.

Colegrave, Sukie (1979). *Uniting Heaven & Earth: A Jungian and Taoist Exploration of Masculine and Feminine in Human Consciousness*. New York: St. Martin's Press.

Coulter, Ann (2006). *Godless: The Church of Liberalism. Crown Publishers.*

Erickson, Milton & Kubie, Lawrence (1979). 'Automatic Drawing in the Treatment of Obsessional Depression' in *Great Cases in Psychotherapy* (eds. Wedding, D. & Corsini, R. J.). Itasca, IL.: F.E. Peacock Publishers, Inc., 283-300.

Hillman, James & Ventura, Michael (1992). *We've Had a Hundred Years of Psychotherapy and the World is Getting Worse*. San Francisco: HarperCollins Publishers.

Kaplan, Aryeh (1997). *Sefer Yetzirah: The Book of Creation in Theory and Practice*. York Beach, ME: Weiser Books.

Kurtz, Ron & Prestera, Hector (1979). *The Body Reveals: An Illustrated Guide to the Psychology of the Body. New York: Harper & Row.*

Kushner, Lawrence (2016). *G-d Was in This Place and I Did Not Know: Finding Self, Spirituality and Ultimate Meaning.* Woodstock, VT: Jewish Lights Publishing

Lofton, Kathryn (2011). *Oprah: The Gospel of an Icon. Oakland, CA: University of California Press.*

Peck, M.S. (1978). *The Road Less Traveled: A New Psychology of Love, Traditional Values and Spiritual Growth. New York: Simon & Shuster*

Peterson, Jordan (1999). *Maps of Meaning: The Architecture of Beliefs.* New York: Routledge

Peterson, Jordan (2017). *12 Rules for Life: An Antidote to Chaos.* New York: Penguin Random House

Peterson, Jordan. Lectures:

"The Psychological Significance of the Biblical Stories," 17 videos

"Personality and its Transformation," 2017, 20 videos

"Maps of Meaning: The Architecture of Belief," 2017, 12 videos

"Maps of Meaning" TVO series

Additional extraneous Peterson YouTube videos.

Poizner, Annette (2003). Graphology in psychotherapy: A Pilot Study exploring clients' and psychotherapists' perceptions of graphology use. Unpublished dissertation.

Poizner, Annette (2004). Graphology in Clinical Practice. *Psychologica,* 24, 1.

Poizner, Annette (2010) The Kabbalistic Tree of Life in Clinical Practice. A paper presented at the 5th North American Conference on Spirituality and Social Work.

Poizner, Annette (2011). Symbolism in Handwriting. *Semiotica*, 185 (1/4), 113-122

Poizner, Annette (2012). *Clinical Graphology: An Interpretive Manual for Mental Health Practitioners*. Springfield, Illinois: Charles C Thomas Publisher.

Poizner, Annette (2019). *A Practical Summary & Workbook for Using Jordan Peterson's Maps of Meaning to Sort Yourself Out.* Toronto: Lobster University Press

Poizner, Annette (2019). *An Illustrated Guide to Using Jordan Peterson's Insights Regarding Divinity & the Map of Meaning.* Toronto: Lobster University Press

Poizner, Annette (2019). *Clean Your Room: An Out-of-the-Box Manual for Lobsters*. Toronto: Lobster University Press

Poizner, Annette (2020). *In Good Standing: Using Jordan Peterson's Insights into the Structure of Self to Sort Yourself Out.* Toronto: Lobster University Press

Poizner, Annette (2019). This Way Up: A Faith-Based Introduction to Jordan Peterson's 'Maps of Meaning'. Toronto: Lobster University Press.

Powers, Robert & Griffith, Jane (1987). *Understanding Life-Style: The Psycho Clarity Process*. Adlerian Psychology Associates, Ltd.

Prager, Dennis (2019). *The Rational Bible: Genesis*. Washington, DC: Regnery Press.

Prager, Dennis. Fireside Chat #85: "Why are there so many mass shootings?"

Project Veritas. "Whistleblower at Google Exposes Plans to Manipulate the 2020 Presidential Election." YouTube Video.

Rohr, Richard (2010). *Falling Upward: A Spirituality for the Two Halves of Life*. Accessible Publishing Systems.

Rovelli, Carlo (2017). *The Order of Time*. Maine: Thorndike.

Sacks, Jonathan (2001). *Radical Then, Radical Now: The Legacy of the World's Oldest Religion*. New York: HarperCollins Publishers.

Schneider, Sarah (2001). *Kabbalistic Writings on the Nature of Masculine & Feminine*. New Jersey: Jason Aronson

Shulman, Bernard & Mosak, Harold (1988) *Manual for Life Style Assessment*. Muncie, Indiana: Accelerated Development, Inc.

Steinsaltz, Adin (2006). *The Thirteen Petaled Rose*. Northvale, New York: Basic Books.

Stone Edition (2001). *The Chumash*. Brooklyn, New York: Mesorah Publications.

Tatz, Akiva (1993). *Living Inspired*. Southfield, Michigan: Targum Press.

Tatz, Akiva (1995). *Worldmask*. Southfield, Michigan: Targum Press.

Wilson, Timothy (2004). *Strangers to Ourselves: Discovering the Adaptive Unconscious*. Cambridge. MA.: Harvard Press

About the Author

Annette Poizner, MSW, Ed.D., RSW

Annette Poizner is a psychotherapist in private practice, a published author and community educator. She completed her Masters degree in Social Work at Columbia University of New York and a Doctorate in Education (specializing in Counseling Psychology) at the University of Toronto. In her clinical practice, she deciphers each client's map of meaning by analyzing dreams and memories. She has specialized training in techniques developed by Dr. Milton Erickson, as well as advanced training in the use of Eye Movement Desensitization Reprocessing (EMDR) and Neuro Linguistic Programming (NLP). She is the co-founder of the Milton H. Erickson Institute of Toronto.

Her work had been featured in dailies across Canada, in trade magazines across North America, and in clinical and academic venues such as at the Canadian Psychological Association annual conference and other professional meetings. She is the author of a textbook published by a leading scholarly publishing house, "*Clinical Graphology: An Interpretive Manual for Mental Health Practitioners.*"

She has published many volumes under the Lobster University Press imprint, including: A *Practical Summary & Workbook for Using Jordan Peterson's Maps of Meaning to Sort Yourself Out, An Illustrated Guide to Using Jordan Peterson's Insights Regarding Divinity and the Map of Meaning to Sort Yourself Out, In Good Standing: Using Jordan Peterson's Insights on the Structure of Self to Sort Yourself Out, This Way Up: A Faith-Based Introduction to Jordan Peterson's Maps of Meaning, Clean Your Room: An Out-of-the-Box Manual for Lobsters* and *From Chaos to Order: A Guide to Jordan Peterson's Worldview*. An upcoming volume, *Yin,*

Yang & You: An Eastern Commentary on Jordan Peterson's 12 Rules for Life will be forthcoming.

You can read more about her work on her blogs: the Times of Israel and Medium.com. She has also been making very short animation videos, intent to communicate soundbites of Peterson's teachings 'in a New York minute'. You can subscribe to the Lobster University Press YouTube channel. You can access many of her other publications on her website, ap.annettepoizner.com. To be advised of the release of the next book in this series or to contact her with feedback about this work (which will be sporadically updated) please email ap@annettepoizner.com or follow the Facebook page, where she will publish ideas, updates and revisions. You will find the webstore at https://macrourl.com/annettestore.

Lobster University Press

Jordan Peterson's *Maps of Meaning: The Architecture of Belief* and the opus of his work, more generally, is vast in scope and complex in nature. I have launched Lobster University Press, named tongue in cheek, for sure, but also with a vision in mind. Peterson relays many ideas that we can unpack, ideas that can help us scale the hierarchy or get a tougher shell to endure life's hardships; maybe even indirectly raise the production of serotonin! The books I publish will focus on specific themes addressed by Peterson in his books and lectures to help readers better integrate the material, expand their 'map of meaning' and tweak that most important of abilities: the capacity to "turn chaos into habitable order!" These works will be the product of discourse and exchange with other Peterson enthusiasts, as we all continue to mine the depth of Peterson's work and explore interesting and helpful applications.

Explore Volume 1 of this series:

A Practical Summary & Workbook for Using Jordan Peterson's Ideas to Sort Yourself Out

By Annette Poizner, MSW, Ed.D., RSW

Less Chaos, More Order!

Whether you are finding Jordan Peterson's "*Maps of Meaning: The Architecture of Belief*" difficult to follow or are simply curious to learn more about the man and his ideas, this summary reviews some of the core insights that characterize Peterson's worldview. Love him or hate him, you might as well get to the crux of what he is saying! With a seasoned psychotherapist as your guide, access Peterson's premises about the nature of reality and how we best live within it. Summaries, summaries of the summaries and reflection points to journal help you digest teachings so you can apply them to your day-to-day life. The second part of this book introduces Alfred Adler's technique for decoding the 'map of meaning' by analyzing a person's 10 earliest memories, further demonstrating how that map manifests in the lives of individuals. This hands-on workbook helps you access vintage Peterson, here presented in a linear style – minus mythology or neurology – so you can zero in on the life advice that has helped many achieve dramatic personal change.*

Please note: the above-mentioned book has 12 chapter. Four of them partly overlap with material in this book, *This Way Up*. The rest of the material is new.

* This book is available in print and large print formats.

Explore Volume 2 of this series:

An Illustrated Guide for Using Jordan Peterson's Insights on Divinity & the Map of Meaning to Sort Yourself Out

By Annette Poizner, MSW, Ed.D., RSW

According to Dr. Jordan Peterson, secular society has overlooked the psychological importance of Divinity, failing to understand the template it provides that helps us flourish. If Peterson is right, we need to review what classic texts tell us about the intricate and specific structure of the G-dhead. Lo and behold, that exact structure pervades creation as a whole, serving as DNA that undergirds the physical world, the human body, the contours of the psyche and more.

In this book, Psychotherapist Annette Poizner first explores Peterson's insights about Divinity, then traces the imprint of Divinity on creation. Exploring the nooks and crannies of our world – surveying diverse areas including graphic design, cultural norms, marketing practices, handedness and more – allows us to see unity, the watermark of Divinity, at the root of creation.

As we explore the central pattern at play, we delve into a visual adventure: learning the structure of Divinity by – believe it or not – analyzing the handwriting of public figures.

Poizner introduces Clinical Graphology, a bona fide European technique for assessing personality, to illustrate how the template of Divinity is our first and only nature. Learning about Oprah, Streisand, Deepak Chopra and others, you will learn about yourself! Explore the profound truths about self and soul that flow each time you pick up a pen . . . en route to our ultimate destination, not to know the rich and famous, but to know G-d and Self. As Poizner writes, "If the Divine infrastructure is intrinsically relevant to us, then societal disinterest and abandonment of the G-d ideal not only banishes G-d but, in some sense, ourselves. We may not know who, or how, to be." Of course, this is exactly Peterson's point.

In a work 15 years in the making, Poizner weaves together the ideas of Jordan Peterson, Jewish Mysticism, Chinese medical theory, Jungian psychology, and 30 years of clinical experience, to survey the interior of our world from a most unique vantage point.

Explore Volume 4 of this series:

Clean Your Room: An Out-of-the-Box Manual for Lobsters

The presidential nominations are underway & Dr. Jordan Peterson nominates you . . . to take bold steps to move your life forward. Ready to turn a new leaf in 2020? Peterson Super Fan Annette Poizner, a therapist, educator and author, extends Peterson's maxim 'Clean your room', making the case for lifestyle changes that may not be on your radar. Contemplating the start of a new decade, Poizner takes instruction from the first beginning on record, as it is conceived in Genesis. Can lessons embedded in that narrative speak to the contemporary lifestyle? Poizner makes the case that old wisdom, peppered with insights from Jordan Peterson, himself, will guide you toward better outcomes. Plan your New Year's Resolutions with the help of a seasoned therapist. Bring your 2020 vision into focus.

Explore Volume 5 of this series:

In Good Standing: Using Jordan Peterson's Insights on the Structure of Self to Sort Yourself Out

Your self has a structure, indirectly alluded to by Dr. Jordan Peterson each time he counsels you to live in alignment, whenever he urges you to stand with your shoulders back and every time he urges you to notice where you're aiming. Even the English 'Personal Pronoun I' alludes to that structure. Look carefully. Back 8 words. See it? It's a straight line.

Therapist Annette Poizner asserts that the archetype of the line, unpacked, delivers a myriad of lessons which can be applied to master the living of life. She will introduce the three-step pattern that underpins reality, expressed in hormonal patterns and stoplights, revealed in classic myths and modern-day acronyms, applied in building structures and hair braiding techniques. In all these, we find a trinity that sits at the root of creation, one referred to in the day-to-day vernacular as "beginning, middle and end," so naming the three points on a straight line. Watch as the contours of reality come into focus, bringing an awareness of a structure that pervades creation . . . and, more importantly, *yourself.*

Poizner, a seasoned clinician, doctoral level practitioner and certified graphologist, will pepper this presentation with references from the Hebrew Bible, other sources *and* with handwritings of prominent public figures! Turns out that we dance with the straight line each time we pick up a pen! We will meet the line in all its manifestations and befriend the archetype that grows us up, helps us stand tall, aims us forward and culminates, ideally, in a singular ego identity. We will come to see that each lie is nothing but a line with a missing piece and will understand that we spell our best success when we embrace the G-d-given archetype and, in so doing, actualize our Divine birthright. We have, after all, been lovingly made in the image of the One, the Only.

With a book designed to change your map of meaning and your perspective of life, you can take Peterson's ideas to the next level. Insights advanced by Rabbi Dr. Akiva Tatz, a Talmudic sage whose scope and intellect matches that of Peterson, will be harnessed by your guide, an author whose psychotherapy practice of 30 years compels a practical vision of what readers need to know to make meaningful and lasting life changes.

Explore Volume 6 of this series:

From Chaos to Order: A Guide to Jordan Peterson's Worldview

Struggling to decipher Jordan Peterson's core worldview when you listen on YouTube? Finding that his mosaic style, fascinating tangents and detours into the mythic realm make him hard to follow? Or maybe you're wondering what the fuss is about and would like a concise introduction to Jordan Peterson's mentality, particularly as it relates to the task of sorting yourself out?

In this book, a seasoned therapist takes you on a tour of Peterson's central ideas. In a clear, linear presentation, Annette Poizner presents Peterson's premises about reality and the specific ways we perceive and organize that reality. She introduces his ideas regarding the map of meaning, outlines his take on how and why our life maps are easily corrupted and follows with his premises about the psychological necessity of the G-d ideal, tracing the sequelae when that ideal is absent, as it is in secular society. Finally, Poizner renders Peterson's map of the life space. We come to see how his rules help readers thrive in reality, given the contours of reality that he discusses. Prepare to see life from a unique, surprising and relevant vantage point.

In providing the scaffolding of Peterson's core arguments, Poizner gifts readers with a big picture that will help them when they read or listen to Peterson, facilitating better comprehension and alleviating some of the inevitable review normally required when working through his material. At the same time, this work bridges material from his two bestselling books, his Biblical lecture series and his University of Toronto courses, depicting overarching themes that emerge across platforms and presenting those clinical insights that have implications for contemporary life. Readers gain a lens through which they can consider their own personal process and are given reflection points that they can use to explore the personal relevance of ideas discussed.

Please note: Four chapters from Volume 1, above, are reprinted in Volume 6.

Explore Volume 7 of this series:

Yin, Yang & You: An Eastern Commentary on Jordan Peterson's 12 Rules for Life

Books that achieve bestseller status are often those that render essential truths, ideas core to our humanity. This is the case, says therapist Annette Poizner, regarding the works of Canadian psychologist Jordan Peterson. In this book, Poizner will analyze Peterson's *12 Rules for Life*, peering through the lens of Traditional Chinese Medicine's Five Element Theory in order to show how his material resonates deeply with a classic and ancient philosophical system.

Five Element Theory posits that five root elements underpin our world, our bodies and even our unique and varied psychologies. The theory renders a detailed understanding of how these elements are best choreographed to achieve a working harmony. Each element governs particular bodily systems but also relates to central psychological attributes. In *Yin, Yang & You*, we will see how Eastern truths shine out of Peterson's teachings, demonstrating why readers best heed Peterson's principles. Learn the infrastructure of your best self and clarify the choreography you can use to achieve it.

In creative chapters ('Learning How to Wok') that take readers on a tour through Peterson's worldview and Eastern premises of health, readers will learn the component parts of their psycho-spiritual constitutions and may come to recognize one particular element that constitutes their unique and personal soul root. Readers will garner lifestyle advice that will help them in their quest to balance the inner elements. We will explore 12 as the number that represents the harmonic integration of the masculine polarity, Yang (associated with the number one) with the feminine polarity, Yin (associated with the number two). In concluding chapters, we will look at the current state of the world, the impact of the Corona virus which has painfully corrected an overriding worldwide Yang excess/imbalance, counterbalancing it with a heavy-handed Yin redress. We will use ancient Chinese wisdom to help us chart a course, as we pursue the long-lost balance. Use Peterson's wisdom in tandem with ancient Eastern principles to find your way forward in the troubling and difficult times ahead.

Due out at a future date.

Explore Volume 8 in this series:

Beyond Chaos: Wrestling with Jordan Peterson's Notion of the Feminine

Thousands report that Jordan Peterson's insights have helped them achieve life-altering change. Yet, by Peterson's own admission, the lion's share of his followers are male. Are there jewels in his opus which could be accessed by women? Psychotherapist Annette Poizner says there are, but first this group needs to better understand what Peterson is actually saying about the feminine. Materials needs to be prepared which will speak to the female sensibility and help dismantle the resistance that prevents some women from approaching Peterson's work.

Does Peterson's talk of 'chaos' as feminine trigger you? Do you disagree with many of his political positions? Poizner asserts that approaching his material with a will to understand yields rewards: readers can benefit from insights, ideas that usefully deviate from the usual societal narrative, while maintaining the license to reject those (political or otherwise) that don't jibe for any given woman. She asserts that women *can* benefit from the materials that Peterson has generously shared online, leveraging insights to achieve significant personal change and delving into constructs of masculine and feminine that are as old as antiquity.

Annette Poizner, a writer, therapist and executive coach, brings unique credentials to the task of introducing Peterson's opus specifically to those women who have, to date, stood in opposition. Born in the 60's, Poizner grew up an avid feminist and remains committed to progress for women. Her clinical work, steeped in Chinese medical theory, the wisdom of the ancient Kabbalah and the psychology of Carl Jung, equips her to perform a rich and detailed rendering of *Yin* and *Yang*, masculine and feminine, towards the end of unpacking Peterson's frame in a way that brings the teachings to life.

Poizner, who herself differs with Peterson on a range of issues, is working to provide a bridge for women who need help getting over the hump: helping them understand where Peterson has been vilified and misquoted, where he advances clinical insight that can be used to make life better and where they can easily agree to disagree with him. In terms of the latter, in so doing women can deliciously host the paradox of life, itself; the paradox that the masculine and feminine polarities are, more than anything else, here to teach us; the paradox, that, more than anything else, represents the central task of life, what we are here to learn.

You will find the webstore at https://macrourl.com/annettestore.

Notes